STUDENT'S
AND WOR
with D

COMBO B A2

TH!NK

SECOND EDITION

Herbert Puchta,
Jeff Stranks &
Peter Lewis-Jones

CAMBRIDGE
UNIVERSITY PRESS

CONTENTS

Vowel sounds: /ʊ/ and /uː/	**Values:** Caring for people and the environment	**Reading** Article: '… just because I didn't want to take a bath.' Website: Gadget reviews **Writing** A paragraph about housework **Listening** Radio programme: advice for young inventors
Strong and weak forms of *was* and *were*	**Values:** Trying, winning and losing **Train to THINK:** Sequencing	**Reading** Magazine article: The world's greatest sporting achievements Web forum: Sporting fails **Writing** An article about a sporting event **Listening** Teens talking about sport

A2 Key for Schools Exam practice

Vowel sounds: /ɪ/ and /aɪ/	**Values:** Valuing our world	**Reading** Magazine article: The wild side of life Blog: Extreme nature! **Writing** An email about an amazing weather event **Listening** Interview with a Kalahari bushman
Voiced /ð/ and unvoiced /θ/ consonants	**Values:** Appreciating other cultures **Train to THINK:** Problem solving	**Reading** Emails: Experiences in foreign countries Letters to a local government website: How can we improve our town? **Writing** An informal email **Listening** Teens making plans

A2 Key for Schools Exam practice

The /h/ consonant sound	**Values:** Exercise and health	**Reading** Magazine article: Changing bodies Blog: Old Wives' Tales **Writing** A phone message **Listening** Conversations about physical problems
Sentence stress	**Values:** Travel broadens the mind **Train to THINK:** Exploring differences	**Reading** Newspaper article: A world record breaker Magazine article: Travelling the world from your sofa! **Writing** An essay: Someone I admire **Listening** A traveller talking to a class

A2 Key for Schools Exam practice

7 SMART LIFE

OBJECTIVES

FUNCTIONS:
giving advice; talking about obligation / lack of obligation; asking for repetition and clarification

GRAMMAR:
have to / don't have to; should / shouldn't; mustn't vs. don't have to

VOCABULARY:
gadgets; housework; expressions with *like*

Get TH!NKING
▶19 Watch the video and think: can you live without your gadgets?

 A ☐

 B ☐

 C ☐

F ☐

 D ☐

 E ☐

READING

1 🔊 7.01 **Match the words in the list with the photos. Write 1–6 in the boxes. Then listen and check.**

> 1 e-reader | 2 digital camera
> 3 flat screen TV | 4 tablet
> 5 laptop | 6 (desktop) computer

2 SPEAKING **Work in pairs. Talk about the objects.**

> I've got a ...   I haven't got a ...

> I think the (laptop) in the photo looks (cool / really new / quite old).

3 SPEAKING **Imagine you could only have one of these things. Which would you choose?**

> I'd choose the ...
> It's important for me because ...
> What about you?

4 🔊 7.02 **Read the sentences and guess the correct answer. Listen and check your answers.**

1 A person who **invents** something *has got an idea and creates something new / has got enough money to buy something new.*

2 If you hear something that is **shocking**, it makes you feel *happy and excited / surprised and upset.*

3 I **researched** the topic *on the camera / on the internet.*

4 What is a **huge** problem for Africa? *There is not enough clean water / There is not enough space for people.*

5 You can get **trachoma** from *dirty water / bad food.*

6 Getting an **eye infection** can make people *deaf / blind.*

7 You buy **gel** in a *plastic bottle / paper bag.*

5 SPEAKING **Work in pairs. Look at the title of the article and the photo on page 67. What do you think the article is about? Compare your ideas with other students.**

6 🔊 7.03 **Read and listen to the article about a young inventor. Are the sentences T (true) or F (false)? Correct the false ones.**

0 Ludwick Marishane is from South Africa.   *T*

1 Ludwick used his laptop to find out more about the world's water situation.

2 Thousands of people get trachoma every year.

3 Trachoma is an illness that can make people blind.

4 Ludwick wanted to help people with trachoma.

5 Ludwick's dream was to help people find clean water.

6 DryBath is helping to save a lot of water all over the world.

7 DryBath is a success.

8 Ludwick wants to invent more things.

'... just because I didn't want to take a bath'

Ludwick Marishane, a young man from South Africa, was with his friends in Limpopo when they started talking about inventing something to put on your skin so you don't have to take a bath. Ludwick thought that this was a great idea. He used his mobile to do some research on the internet, and he found some shocking facts.

Millions of people around the world haven't got clean water. This is a huge problem because dirty water can create terrible illnesses. One of them is trachoma: thousands of people all over the world get trachoma every year. They wash their faces with dirty water, get an infection and sometimes become blind. To stop trachoma, people don't have to take expensive medication. They don't have to take pills. They don't have to have injections. They have to wash their faces with clean water. That's it.

Ludwick started thinking. He wanted to make something to help people in parts of the world where it's difficult to find clean water. He did more research on his mobile, and he did more thinking. Ludwick had a plan. He wanted to make a gel for people to put on their skin so they don't have to take a bath. He wrote the formula for the gel on his mobile phone. When he was at university, he never stopped thinking about his invention. He started to talk to other people about it,

and three years later the dream came true. He made the gel and called it 'DryBath'. It looks like any other gel, but it isn't. This gel saves lives!

Ludwick Marishane is the winner of lots of prizes. People call him 'one of the brightest young men in the world'. He is very happy about his success. DryBath is helping people to be healthy. And DryBath also helps to save water. That's important in many parts of the world where it's difficult to find clean water. Now he wants to invent other things, and he wants to help other young people to become inventors, too.

TH!NK values

Caring for people and the environment

7 **Match the values in the list with the sentences in the speech bubbles. Write a–d in the boxes.**

a caring about the environment
b caring about the quality of your work
c caring about your appearance
d caring about other people

1 *The water in a lot of rivers and lakes is not clean.* ☐

2 *I need to wash my hair. It's dirty.* ☐

3 *Are you feeling cold? I can give you my jumper.* ☐

4 *Can you switch off the radio, please? I'm doing my homework.* ☐

8 **SPEAKING Work in pairs. Ask and answer questions about Ludwick Marishane. Try and find as many answers as possible.**

*Does he care about the environment?
his appearance?
the quality of his work?
other people?*

He cares about the environment because DryBath helps to save water.

GRAMMAR
have to / don't have to

1 **Complete the sentences from the article on page 67 with *have to* and *don't have to*.**

1 To stop trachoma, people _____ take expensive medication.

2 They _____ wash their faces with clean water.

2 **Complete the rule and the table.**

> **RULE:** Use [1]_____ to say 'this is necessary'.
> Use [2]_____ to say 'this isn't necessary'.

Positive	Negative
I/you/we/they [0] *have to* help.	I/you/we/they don't have to help.
He/she/it [1]_____ help.	He/she/it [2]_____ help.

Questions	Short answers
[3]_____ I/you/we/they have to help?	Yes, I/you/we/they do. No, I/you/we/they don't.
[4]_____ he/she/it have to help?	Yes, he/she/it [5]_____ . No, he/she/it [6]_____ .

3 **Match the sentences with the pictures.**

1 The bus leaves in 20 minutes. He has to hurry.

2 The bus leaves in 20 minutes. He doesn't have to hurry.

4 **Complete the sentences with *have to* / *has to* or *don't* / *doesn't have to*.**

1 Our teacher doesn't like mobile phones. We _____ switch them off during lessons.

2 I know that I _____ work hard for this test! You _____ tell me!

3 Ann's ill. She _____ stay home.

4 Your room's a mess! You _____ tidy it up.

5 His English is perfect. He _____ study for exams.

6 I can hear you very well. You _____ shout!

→ *workbook page 64*

VOCABULARY
Gadgets

5 🔊 **7.04** **Match the words with the photos. Then listen, check and repeat.**

> 1 satnav | 2 MP3 player | 3 torch | 4 games console
> 5 remote control | 6 coffee machine | 7 calculator
> 8 docking station | 9 hair dryer | 10 headphones

6 **How important are these gadgets for you? Make a list from 1 to 10 (1= most important, 10 = not important at all).**

7 **SPEAKING** **Work in pairs. Compare your ideas and tell your partner how often you use these gadgets.**

> *I often use ...*
>
> *I use my ... almost every day.*
>
> *What about you?*
>
> *I rarely use ...*

→ *workbook page 66*

🎧 LISTENING

8 SPEAKING **Look at the pictures of different inventions. Match them with the phrases. Then make sentences to explain what the inventions are. Compare your ideas.**

1 not tidy up room / have got robot
2 machine help / ride bike up a hill
3 invention help homework / more time for friends
4 machine can get places around the world / 10 seconds

 A
 C
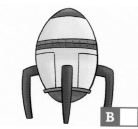 B
 D

The girl in picture A has got a cool machine. It helps her to ride her bike up a hill.

9 🔊 7.05 **An expert is talking to a group of teenagers about becoming an inventor. Match the sentence halves to find out what the person says. Then listen and check.**

1 Many people think that you have to be older ☐
2 The point is that he invented something ☐
3 It's not a good idea ☐
4 After leaving school, you should ☐

a to make people's lives easier.
b to become an inventor.
c get a job first before trying to become an inventor.
d to work on more than one invention at a time.

10 🔊 7.05 **Complete the expert's answers with *should* or *shouldn't*. Listen again and check.**

1 You _____ start with an idea to help other people.
2 You _____ think 'How can I get rich?'
3 You _____ only talk to people that you can trust about your ideas.
4 You _____ work on all the ideas at the same time.
5 You _____ get a job and invent things as a hobby.
6 You _____ make sure that you've got a job.

🄖 GRAMMAR
should / shouldn't

11 **Look at the sentences in Exercise 10. Match the sentence halves.**

> **RULE:**
> 1 Use ***should*** to say   a 'It's not a good idea.'
> 2 Use ***shouldn't*** to say   b 'It's a good idea.'

12 **Use *should / shouldn't* and a word from each list to give advice to these people.**

> ~~take~~ | go to | eat | drink | read
>
> ~~medicine~~ | book anymore | bed
> any more cake | some water

0 I've got a headache. *You should take some medicine.*
1 I'm really thirsty. _____
2 My eyes are tired. _____
3 I'm tired. _____
4 I feel sick. _____

⟶ **workbook page 64**

WordWise: Expressions with *like*

13 **Match the sentences.**

1 This chicken isn't very good. ☐
2 Someone's talking. Who is it? ☐
3 Let's buy her a present. ☐
4 He's a really nice guy. ☐
5 What's that animal? ☐

a Like what? A poster perhaps?
b Yes, he's just like his sister, she's nice, too.
c I'm not sure. It looks like a rabbit, but it isn't.
d That's right. It tastes like fish!
e It sounds like Jim.

14 **Complete the dialogues using a phrase with *like*.**

1 A I forgot my homework.
  B I'm _____ . Mine's at home, too.
2 A Here's a photo of my sister.
  B Wow. She really _____ you!
3 A We should do some exercise.
  B _____ ? Go for a walk?
4 A Let's go to the cinema.
  B That _____ a great idea.

⟶ **workbook page 66**

1 SPEAKING **Work in pairs. Look at the pictures and think about what the machines do. Then choose one of the two machines and talk about it.**

> I think it's called ...
> It's a cool machine because ...
> It helps with ...

2 🔊 7.06 **Read and listen to these product reviews on a website from the year 2066. What do the machines do?**

Are you tired of choosing a cool outfit to wear for special occasions? Well, now you don't have to!

The all-new Trendy-wise is easy to use and you don't have to be trendy to use it. However, before you can use it, you have to take photos of all the clothes in your wardrobe. And you mustn't forget to take photos of all your shoes and socks, too. Then all you have to do is click on a photo of, for example, a blue T-shirt. The Trendy-wise selects photos of trousers or skirts, shoes, socks, etc., from your wardrobe to go with this T-shirt. Each time it creates a different outfit for you and the outfits are all very trendy. Oh, I almost forgot! You also have to type in the kind of event/occasion, for example: a concert or a birthday party.

Do you sometimes have bad dreams? Do you wake up scared or unhappy? Yes? Then you should buy the DreamCatcher.

This is how it works: Put the machine on your head before you go to bed. Tell it what you want or don't want by speaking into the microphone – for example: 'I want dreams where I win a singing competition' or 'I don't want dreams about falling.' When you are asleep, DreamCatcher will follow your dreams and make sure you get what you want. Imagine that in your dream you do something dangerous. DreamCatcher will make sure you're safe. Here's an example. Let's say you start to climb a high mountain. You don't have to worry because the DreamCatcher will make you walk back down again.

But you mustn't use the machine every night. It will only work every three days.

3 **Read the reviews again and answer the questions.**

1 What do you have to do before you can use the Trendy-wise?
2 What mustn't you forget to do?
3 What other thing do you have to do?
4 How does the DreamCatcher work?
5 Let's say you have a dangerous dream. How does the DreamCatcher help you?
6 What mustn't you do when you use the DreamCatcher?

Grammar rap!
▶20

🔍 **GRAMMAR**
mustn't / don't have to

4 **Complete the sentences from the reviews.**

1 You _____ be trendy to use the new Trendy-wise.
2 You _____ forget to take photos of all your shoes and socks, too.

5 **Complete the rule with *mustn't* or *don't have to*.**

> **RULE:** Use [1]_____ to say 'it's not necessary'.
> Use [2]_____ to say 'don't do it! I'm telling you not to!'

6 **Match sentences (1–2) with (a–b).**

1 You don't have to go swimming.
2 You mustn't go swimming.

a There are sharks.
b You can do something else if you prefer.

7 **Complete the sentences with *mustn't* or *don't have to*.**

1 A The film starts soon. We _____ be late.
  B Don't worry. I'm ready now.
2 A I'm so thirsty.
  B Stop! You _____ drink that!
3 A I'm sorry I can't join you.
  B That's fine. You _____ come.
4 A Sorry, I can't stay. I'm in a hurry.
  B No problem. You _____ wait for me.
5 A I can't swim very well.
  B Then you really _____ swim here. The water's deep.

→ workbook page 65

PRONUNCIATION
Vowel sounds: /ʊ/ and /uː/ Go to page 121.

A

B

C

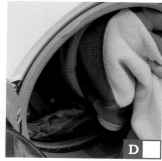
D

VOCABULARY
Housework

8 🔊 7.09 **Match the words with the photos. Write 1–10 in the boxes. Listen and check. Then listen again and repeat.**

> **1** vacuum the floor | **2** tidy up | **3** do the ironing
> **4** do the shopping | **5** set / clear the table
> **6** do the washing-up (wash up) | **7** make the beds
> **8** do the cooking | **9** do the washing
> **10** load / empty the dishwasher

→ workbook page 66

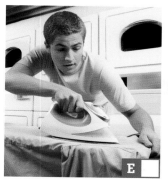
E

F

SPEAKING

9 **Read the questions. Make notes.**

1 What do you have to do at home: tidying, shopping, cooking, etc.?
2 What don't you have to do?
3 What should parents / children do at home?

10 **Plan what you are going to say. Use these phrases.**

> I have to ... I think / don't think that's fair.

> I don't have to ... I'm quite happy about that.

> But it would be OK for me to do that.

> I think ... should do the same amount of work.
> It's not fair that ...
> Mothers / Fathers should do more work because ...

G

H

I

J

11 **Work in pairs or small groups. Compare your ideas about housework.**

WRITING
A paragraph about housework

12 **Ask your partner these questions and make notes. Then write a paragraph.**

1 What do you have to do at home?
2 What don't you have to do at home?
3 When do you have to do housework?
4 What do you feel about this housework?

Kate hates clearing the table, but she has to do it every evening. She also has to vacuum her bedroom floor once a week. She doesn't have to do ...

1 🔊 **7.10** **Look at the photo. What is the woman looking at? Why is she upset? Listen and read to check.**

Ryan: All right, Mum?

Mum: No, not really, Ryan, I really need you to help me.

Ryan: Sorry, Mum? What did you say?

Mum: I said I need some help, Ryan. There are so many things to do in this house.

Ryan: Like what?

Mum: Well, this washing up, for a start. Look at all this! It's terrible. So, can you do it for me before you go out, please?

Ryan: No chance, Mum! I'm leaving soon and I've got lots of things to do. I'm really busy, you know.

Mum: What do you mean?

Ryan: Well, homework and stuff. You know.

Mum: OK. Never mind. You don't have to help me. But I have to leave soon. I have a meeting with a new client. I mustn't be late.

Ryan: Oh, OK. Sorry, Mum. Don't worry. I can do it. Leave it all to me, OK?

Mum: Are you sure?

Ryan: Absolutely. You go now and leave everything to me.

Mum: OK, thanks Ryan. You're a good boy! Bye!

Ryan: OK, well it *is* a lot of washing up, and perhaps I should clean the kitchen, too. But the game starts right now and there's no TV in here. Hmm. Problem. Some creative thinking is needed. Well, it's easy of course. Get my phone. Do live streaming of the game. Put the phone next to the sink. And great! Off we go. And the game's starting. Come on United. Argh, no! That's my new phone!

2 🔊 **7.10** **Read and listen again to the dialogue and answer the questions.**

1 How do you think Ryan's mum is feeling at the start of the dialogue?

2 Why can't Ryan hear his mum?

3 Why doesn't Ryan want to help his mum?

4 Where do you think Ryan should put his phone?

Phrases for fluency

3 **Find the expressions 1–5 in the story. Who says them? How do you say them in your language?**

0 No chance.   *Ryan*

1 … and stuff.   _____

2 Never mind.   _____

3 Absolutely.   _____

4 So, … ?   _____

5 All right … ?   _____

4 **Complete the dialogue with the expressions in Exercise 3.**

A ¹_____ , Dan? Do you want to come round tonight? We can play computer games ²_____ .

B ³_____ . I love computer games, they're awesome!

A Can you bring your new laptop?

B ⁴_____ . It's my brother's. I can't take it.

A ⁵_____ . We can use mine.

B ⁶_____ , is seven o'clock OK?

 FUNCTIONS
Asking for repetition and clarification

> **KEY LANGUAGE**
>
> What do you mean?   Sorry?   Like what?

5 **Write the expressions from the Key Language box next to their definitions.**

a Say that again. _____

b What are you trying to say? _____

c Give me an example. _____

6 **Complete the extracts from the conversations with the words from Exercise 5.**

Mum   Ryan, I really need you to help me.

Ryan   ¹_____ , Mum? What did you say?

Mum   There are so many things to do in this house.

Ryan   ²_____ ?

Ryan   I'm really busy, you know.

Mum   ³_____ ?

ROLE PLAY **A phone call**

Work in pairs. Student A: Go to page 127. Student B: Go to page 128. Take two or three minutes to prepare. Then have a conversation.

LIFE COMPETENCIES

Everybody has problems to solve. Sometimes the problems are big, and sometimes they are small, but it's always a good idea to think of all the possibilities before we decide what to do.

Solving problems

PROBLEM

1 ▶ 21 **Watch the vlog and complete the sentence.**

'Someone once said that life is just a series of _____ looking for _____'.

Do you think the sentence is true? Why is problem solving important?

2 ▶ 21 **Watch again and complete the notes.**

What to vlog about?

1 – Topic: Empathy

For	Against
2 – It's interesting	5 – _____
3 – _____	
4 – _____	

6 – Topic: _____

For	Against
7 – _____	9 – Not really 'Life Lessons'
8 – _____	

TIPS FOR SOLVING PROBLEMS

- When you have a problem, spend some time trying to think of all the possible solutions.
- When you have all the possible solutions, think about the positives and negatives for each solution.
- After listing the positives and negatives, choose what you think the best solution is.
- Remember sometimes there is no good solution and you have to choose the one that is least bad.

3 **Read the conversation. What is Ben's problem?**

Andy Hey, Ben. What are you doing?

Ben Hello, Andy. I'm thinking about how to go to school next week.

Andy Why?

Ben My mum's car isn't working, so we have to find another way. One idea is getting the bus.

Andy Good idea. The bus is fast, so you can get to school early. So, can we go out now?

Ben Hang on! I can see here that the bus goes at 7.10, so I have to get up at … 6. No chance! Also, I need to take my little sister to her school and I don't want to be at school an hour early.

Andy So why don't you walk? You can take Annie to school, walk from there to my house and then we can go to school together.

Ben Sounds good, but I'm not so sure. Annie's school is a long way from your house. And I don't want to arrive at school late, but I can't leave Annie at her school at 8 am. It's not open until 8.15.

Andy OK, so the bus is a no, and walking a no, too? How about going on your bikes? You can cycle with Annie to her school at 8.15 and have time to get to school about 10 minutes early.

Ben Good idea! But Annie hasn't got a bike.

4 **Ben and Andy think of three solutions. What are they? What are the positives and the negatives about each solution?**

5 SPEAKING **With your partner, think of another solution to Ben's problem. What are the positives and negatives about your solution?**

6 SPEAKING **Explain your solution to the rest of the class. Who has the best solution?**

Me and my world

7 **Answer the questions.**

a Think of a small, medium and large problem that you have.

b Who can you talk to about these problems?

c Have you got ideas about how to solve them?

8 A QUESTION OF SPORT

OBJECTIVES

FUNCTIONS:
talking about sports; talking about feelings; talking about ongoing past events, sequencing events

GRAMMAR:
past continuous; past continuous vs. past simple; *when* and *while*

VOCABULARY:
sport and sports verbs; adverbs of sequence

Get TH!NKING

▶22

Watch the video and think: what can you learn from winning and losing?

A

B

C

D

E

F

📖 READING

1 **Match the words in the list with the photos. Write 1–6 in the boxes.**

> **1** basketball | **2** horse racing | **3** gymnastics
> **4** athletics | **5** swimming | **6** tennis

2 **Which sport(s) in Exercise 1 has these things?**

> a ball | a race | a track | water
> bars | a net | a match | a rider

3 **Name other sports in English.**

4 **Which sports are popular in your country? Which ones do you like? Write P (popular) and/or L (like) next to each photo.**

5 SPEAKING **Compare your ideas with a partner.**

> *Basketball is popular here, but I don't like it very much.*

> *I like tennis and it's very popular here.*

6 **Look at the photos on page 75. Which sports are the stories about?**

7 ◁)) 8.01 **Read and listen to the article and check your answers.**

8 **Read the article again. Are the sentences T (true) or F (false)? Correct the false ones.**

1 Usain Bolt won both the 100m and 200m gold medals at three Olympic Games.
2 Bolt won all his gold medals running on his own.
3 Bolt was world champion 11 times.
4 Nadia Comaneci was 16 years old when she got the perfect score.
5 The scoreboard didn't show Comaneci's score correctly.
6 Comaneci scored 10.00 six times at the Montreal Olympics.
7 Some people thought it was impossible to run a mile in four minutes.
8 Roger Bannister did not win a medal at the 1952 Olympic Games.

THE WORLD'S GREATEST SPORTING ACHIEVEMENTS

The world of sport is full of wonderful moments. Here are our top three.

⭐ The triple double

The starting gun went off. Suddenly, eight athletes were flying down the track in Rio de Janeiro's Olympic Stadium. Less than 20 seconds later the race was over. Usain Bolt was walking around the stadium with the Jamaican flag over his shoulders – he was a double Olympic champion … again! Four years earlier, at the 2012 London Olympics, he became the first man to win a gold medal in both the 100m and 200m sprint at a second Olympic Games (he won them both at the 2008 Beijing Olympics, too). In Rio, he did it for a third time. As well as his eight Olympic gold medals (he won the other two in relay races with other teammates), Bolt also won 11 world championships and currently holds the world record for the 100m and 200m. He is one of the greatest sprinters in history.

⭐ The perfect ten

Everyone was looking at 15-year-old Romanian gymnast Nadia Comaneci as she left the bars, flew through the air and landed perfectly on the ground. She turned round. The crowd was cheering. Everyone was waiting nervously for the judges' score. Then it came. The scoreboard was showing '1.00'. The crowd was confused. But then the organisers explained. The makers of the scoreboards thought it was impossible to get a perfect score of 10. The boards were not able to show '10.00'. So, on 18 July 1976, at the Montreal Olympics, Nadia made history when she became the first gymnast ever to get a perfect ten. She got six more 'perfect scores' at the games and won three gold medals, making her one of the best athletes in her sport of all time.

⭐ The four-minute mile

It was the final lap. Roger Bannister was running fast, but could he really become the first person to run a mile in under four minutes? A minute later, he was lying exhausted on the ground. Then, there was an announcement of his time: '3 minutes, 59.4 seconds.' The crowd went crazy.

Before 6 May 1954, experts said that a four-minute mile was impossible to run. Roger showed them that they were wrong. He planned to stop running after the 1952 Summer Olympics, but there he only came in fourth place. Without a medal, Roger wanted to show how good he was. In 1954, he did exactly that.

TH!NK *values*

Trying, winning and losing

9 **Think about these sentences. Which do you agree with most?**

1 When you play sport, you should always try your hardest.
2 Having fun is more important than winning.
3 No one remembers the person who finishes second.
4 Getting physical exercise is more important than winning trophies.
5 Sport is the most important thing in life.

10 **SPEAKING** **Work in pairs. Compare your ideas with a partner.**

> *I agree with number 1 the most. What about you?*

@ GRAMMAR
Past continuous

1 **Complete the sentences from the article on page 75 with the words in the correct form. Then choose the correct words to complete the rule.**

> cheer | fly | lie | run

1 Eight athletes _____ down the track.
2 The crowd _____ .
3 Roger Bannister _____ fast.
4 A minute later, he _____ exhausted on the ground.

> **RULE:** Use the past continuous to talk about
> [5]*completed actions* / *actions in progress* at a certain time in the past.

2 **Find more examples of the past continuous in the article on page 75. Then complete the table.**

Positive	Negative
I/he/she/it [1]_____ working.	I/he/she/it [3]_____ (was not) working.
You/we/they [2]_____ working.	You/we/they weren't (were not) working.

Questions	Short answers
[4]_____ I/he/she/it working?	Yes, I/he/she/ it [6]_____ . No, I/he/she/it [7]_____ (was not).
[5]_____ you/we/they working?	Yes, you/we/they/ [8]_____ . No, you/we/they [9]_____ (were not).

> **PRONUNCIATION**
> Strong and weak forms of *was* and *were*
> Go to page 121. 🎧

3 **Yesterday the sports teacher was late. What were the students doing when he got there? Complete the sentences with the correct form of the verbs.**

0 Lucy ____*was talking*____ (talk) on her phone.
1 Daniel and Sophie _____ (play) basketball.
2 Samuel _____ (read) a book.
3 Ken and Sarah _____ (climb) up the ropes.
4 Lisa _____ (not think) about sports. She _____ (dream) about a day on the beach.
5 Andy and Matt _____ (not do) any sports. They _____ (look) at photos on Andy's tablet.

4 **Complete the dialogues with the past continuous form of the verbs.**

1 A What _____ (you/do) yesterday when we phoned you?
  B I _____ (wait) for my mum in town. And it was horrible because it _____ (rain)!
2 A Why didn't you answer when I phoned you?
  B I _____ (cook) my lunch.
3 A Was it a good game yesterday?
  B Well, the beginning was fine. We _____ (play) well and we _____ (win). But then they scored four goals!
4 A _____ (you/watch) TV when I called last night?
  B No, I wasn't. I _____ (read) a magazine.

> → *workbook page 72*

A F B G C H D I E J

Az VOCABULARY
Sport and sports verbs

5 **Match the words in the list with the photos. Write 1–10 in the boxes.**

> **1** sailing | **2** diving | **3** golf | **4** gymnastics
> **5** rock climbing | **6** rugby | **7** snowboarding
> **8** skiing | **9** volleyball | **10** windsurfing

6 Answer the questions.

1 Two of the sports in Exercise 5 have *players* and a *team*. Which ones are they?

2 Seven of the sports in Exercise 5 add *-er* or *-or* for the people who do them. Which ones are they?

3 What do we call someone who does gymnastics?

7 We use different verbs for different kinds of sports. Read the rule and then complete the table with the sports in Exercise 5.

> **RULE:** *play* + game (e.g., *football*)
> *go* + *-ing* (e.g., *running*)
> *do* + activity (e.g., *athletics*)

play	go	do
football	running	athletics

8  **SPEAKING** Work in groups. Answer the questions about the sports in Exercise 5.

Which sports …

1 are team sports?
2 are dangerous?
3 are water sports?
4 are in the Winter Olympics?
5 are expensive?
6 are difficult to play or do?

→ workbook page **74**

🎧 LISTENING

9 🔊 **8.04** Five teenagers were asked the question: 'How do you feel about sport?' Listen and draw the correct emoji for each sport they mention.

They really like it. 😊	It's OK for them. 😐	They don't like it. 😞

	Gemma	Andy	Tracey	Paul	Ryan
football					
swimming					
running					
skateboarding					
gymnastics					
skiing					
tennis					

10 🔊 **8.04** Listen again. Who expresses these ideas? Write the name.

1 I practise a lot.
_____

2 I am not competitive.
_____

3 I like doing things alone.
_____

4 I'm learning another sport.
_____

5 I can't do my sport at school.
_____

11 **SPEAKING** Work in pairs. Which of the five teenagers are you like? Tell your partner.

> *I'm like Ryan. I love all sports.*

> *I'm like Andy because I prefer individual sports.*

Look 👁

You can use *like* to say that you have similar interests to somebody or that you have the same abilities.
Sarah's **like** Greg. She loves tennis.
Matt's **like** his brother. They're both good at gymnastics.

⚙ FUNCTIONS
Talking about feelings

12 You are going to answer the question: 'How do you feel about sport?' List some sports you want to talk about.

running, football, swimming, surfing

13 What do you want to say about each sport? Mark them ✓ for positive comments; and ✗ for negative ones.

running ✗   football ✗   swimming ✓   surfing ✓

14 Think about why you put ✓ or ✗. Look at the words and ideas in Exercise 8. Use these words and / or other words you know.

running ✗ boring   football ✗ team sport
swimming ✓ fun   surfing ✓ difficult and fun

15 Work in pairs. Ask each other: 'How do you feel about sport?'

> *How do you feel about sport?*

> *Well, I don't like running because it's boring. But swimming is fun and I love surfing because it's fun and it's difficult to do.*

Sporting fails 👎

Professional athletes need their bodies to be in excellent condition. They train hours every day to achieve this. Sometimes it only takes one small mistake to spoil all that hard work. In 2011, for example, French golfer Thomas Levet won the French Open. He was so happy that he jumped in a lake and broke his leg. And American skier Lindsey Vonn cut her hand badly while she was opening a glass bottle to celebrate winning at the 2009 World Championships.

We know you're not professionals, but we want you to tell us all about your silliest sporting accidents.

1 Last year, I was playing volleyball for my school team. I jumped up high and hit the ball really hard. At first, I thought it was a really good shot, but I soon found out it wasn't. The ball hit the post at the side of the net: then it hit me in the face and knocked me to the floor. I had a big purple bruise on my face and I couldn't play the rest of the game. *Liam*

2 When I was 13, I played for the school rugby team and we won the schools championship. A few days later, there was a big celebration. All the students were there to watch as we walked on to the stage to get medals from the headmistress. I got my medal, but when I was leaving the stage, I tripped and fell down the steps. Luckily, I wasn't hurt, but I was really, really embarrassed. *Connor*

3 A few days ago I was skateboarding down my road when I saw my best friend. I shouted to him and started waving. While I was waving, I rode into a lamppost and fell off. My leg was hurting really badly and I couldn't move. After ten minutes, my friend called an ambulance. Finally, they took me to hospital. The doctor there told me my leg was broken. Now I can't skateboard for at least six months, and I have to miss the local championships. *Eve*

A

B

C

📖 READING

1 **Look at the pictures. What do you think is happening in each one?**

2 🔊 8.05 **Read and listen to the stories and match them with the pictures. Write the numbers 1–3 in the boxes.**

3 **Read the forum again. Answer the questions.**
  1 Why did the golfer jump into a lake?
  2 How did the skier cut her hand?
  3 After Liam hit the ball, what did it do?
  4 What was Connor doing when he fell?
  5 Why can't Eve skateboard for the next six months?

4 **SPEAKING** **How funny do you think these stories are? Give each one a number from 0–5 (0 = not funny at all, 5 = very, very funny). Compare your ideas with a partner.**

Train to TH!NK

Sequencing

5 **Look at the lists. Put them in a logical order.**
  1 morning – night – afternoon – evening
  2 tomorrow – today – next week – yesterday
  3 Saturday – Wednesday – Monday – Friday
  4 have lunch – come home – go to school – wake up
  5 baby – adult – child – teenager
  6 first half – kick-off – half-time – second half

6 **SPEAKING** **Compare your ideas with other students. Are they the same or different?**

G GRAMMAR
Past continuous vs. past simple

7 Look at these sentences from the stories on page 78. Which verbs are in the past continuous and which verbs are in the past simple?

1 Lindsey Vonn cut her hand badly while she was opening a glass bottle.
2 When I was leaving the stage, I tripped and fell down the steps.
3 I was skateboarding down my road when I saw my best friend.
4 While I was waving, I rode into a lamppost.

8 Look at the diagram. Which part tells us the background action? Which part says what happened at one moment? Complete the rule.

> I **was skateboarding** down the road.
> ——————————————————→
> I **saw** my best friend. ↑

> **RULE:** Use the ¹_____ to talk about background actions in the past, and the ²_____ for actions which happened at one moment (and sometimes interrupted the background action).

9 Complete the sentences. Use the past continuous or past simple form of the verbs.

0 He ___*was running*___ (run) and he suddenly _____*felt*_____ (feel) a pain in his leg.
1 The ball _____ (hit) me while I _____ (watch) a bird.
2 Jenny _____ (sail) with her father when she _____ (see) some dolphins.
3 He _____ (chase) the ball and he _____ (fall) over.
4 When I _____ (look) out of the window, it _____ (snow).

when and while

10 Look at Exercise 9. Complete the rule.

> **RULE:** We often use *when* before the past ¹_____ and *while* before the past ²_____ .

11 Complete the sentences with the correct form of the verbs. Use past continuous for the longer activity and past simple for the shorter one.

> arrive | go | have (x2) | ~~ring~~
> see | talk | walk | watch | ~~write~~

0 I _____*was writing*_____ an email.
My phone _____*rang*_____ .
1 Alex and Sue _____ a film. Their friends _____ .
2 Marco _____ breakfast.
He _____ a great idea.
3 Cristina _____ on the phone.
Her father _____ out.
4 They _____ in the mountains.
They _____ a strange bird.

12 Join the sentences in Exercise 11 in two different ways. Use *when* and *while*.

→ workbook page 73

Az VOCABULARY
Adverbs of sequence

13 Match the parts of the sentences.

1 At first,   a 15 minutes, they phoned 999.
2 Then   b they took me to hospital.
3 After   c I thought it was a really good shot.
4 Finally,   d it came straight back towards me.

14 Complete the story with the words in Exercise 13.

¹_____ , I was very nervous.
²_____ the starter fired the gun.

³_____ ten seconds, I crossed the finish line and won! I was the world champion!

⁴_____ the photographers took photos of me.
⁵_____ an hour, they gave me the gold medal.

⁶_____ , I woke up.

→ workbook page 74

TH!NK
The wonderful world of sport

Culture

1 **Look at the photos and answer the question. Then say what you think the article is about. Where can you see the following things?**
- people climbing
- a net
- camels
- a chess board

2 🔊 8.06 **Read and listen to the article. Match the pictures with the sports (1–4).**

3 SPEAKING **Which sport do you like most? Which do you not like? Compare your ideas with others in the class.**

The wonderful **world** of sport

Sports such as football, tennis and golf are popular all over the world with millions of people playing them or watching them on TV. But there are also many unusual sports that are not so well known. Here are four interesting examples.

1 Every year, on a small Chinese island, thousands of people arrive to celebrate a very special event: the Cheung Chau bun festival. The highlight of the festival is a race to the top of a very strange mountain. The mountain is made of metal and covered with a type of traditional Chinese bun. Spectators watch as three teams compete to see how many buns they can take from the mountain. The climb can be quite dangerous and people who want to take part must take a special training course.

2 Camel racing is a popular sport in many countries around the world, including Mongolia and Australia. But it is especially popular in the Middle East and each year, from late October to early April, many big races take place in countries such as the United Arab Emirates. As many as 70 camels race along sandy desert tracks for up to 16 km. The owners of the camels drive by the side of the animals shouting at them to run faster and cross the finish line before the others.

3 Bossaball is a very modern sport that was first played in 2005. It started in Spain, but it was the idea of a Belgian man called Filip Eyckmans. He wanted to create a sport that mixed together football, gymnastics, volleyball and the Brazilian music of bossa nova. There are two trampolines with a net between them. The idea is for one team to hit the ball over the net and the other team to try and hit it back. The trampolines let the players jump very high, making the sport very exciting to watch. The sport is already popular in many countries around the world, including Brazil, Mexico, Turkey, Singapore and Saudi Arabia.

4 Chess boxing was the invention of Dutch artist Iepe Rubingh. His original idea was to create a piece of performance art, but it was so popular that it soon became a sport played in countries all over the world. The game is quite simple. Two contestants compete against each other at chess and boxing. Each round of chess is followed by a round of boxing with a break of a minute between each round to give the players time to put on or take off their gloves. The first person to win either the chess match or the boxing match wins the game.

A

B

C

D

4 Read the article again and answer the questions. Why …

1 do thousands of people go to a Chinese island every year?
2 do people climb the metal mountain?
3 do camel owners drive beside the camels and shout?
4 did Filip Eyckmans create bossaball?
5 is bossaball exciting to watch?
6 do people playing chess boxing stop for one minute?

5 **VOCABULARY** There are eight highlighted words in the article. Match the words with these meanings. Write the words.

0 are involved in an activity or sport — *take part*
1 the people who try to win a race / game / quiz (etc.) — _____
2 a short time between two things — _____
3 happen — _____
4 a competition to see who is the fastest at something — _____
5 people who watch a race or game — _____
6 to go across from one side of something to another — _____
7 a small, sweet cake (usually round) — _____

WRITING
An article about a sporting event

1 **INPUT** Read Joanna's article in a school magazine about going to an important tennis match. Answer the questions.

1 Who did Joanna go with?
2 Who did Joanna think would win?
3 Who won?
4 What did Joanna do after the match?

2 Find these words in the article. What does each word describe? Why does Joanna use them?

0 lucky — *my family*
1 full — _____
2 excited — _____
3 quite easy — _____
4 great — _____
5 fantastic — _____

3 **ANALYSE** Look at the three paragraphs of Joanna's article. Match the paragraphs with the contents.

Paragraph 1   a after the event
Paragraph 2   b introduction to the event
Paragraph 3   c details of the event (the match itself)

Home   About   Latest news

(1) Last Saturday was the final of the women's singles at the Wimbledon Championships, played (of course) at the All England Club (Wimbledon). My family were lucky enough to get tickets. When we got there, we went to the court and found our seats. Of course, the stadium was full and everyone was very excited. It was brilliant!

(2) At ten to two, the players came out: Venus Williams from the US and Garbiñe Muguruza from Spain. At first, I was sure Williams was going to win because she was a five-times Wimbledon champion, but as the match continued, it was clear that I was wrong. Both players played really well and after almost an hour, the exciting first set ended: 7-5 to Muguruza. Could 37-year-old Williams come back? No. She started to look tired and to play badly. The second set was quite easy for Muguruza, and after 20 minutes, she won the set 6–0 and won the match. At the age of 23, she was the new Wimbledon champion. The crowd stood and clapped and cheered. And then Muguruza got the trophy.

(3) After the match, we looked around a bit and then went home. We had a great time. The match was very exciting and it was fantastic to see a big sports event 'live'.

4 **PLAN** Think of a sports event that you went to or would like to go to. Answer the questions.

1 When is / was the event?
2 Where is / was it?
3 What is / was the atmosphere like (the crowd, the noise, etc.)?
4 What happens / happened at the event (players / goals / winners, etc.)?
5 How did / would you feel after the event (happy / tired / excited / unhappy)?

5 **PRODUCE** Write an article for a school magazine (about 120–150 words) about the sports event. Use Joanna's article and the language above to help you.

A2 Key for Schools

READING AND WRITING
Part 1: 3-option multiple choice

→ **workbook page 71**

1 **For each question, choose the correct answer.**

A The bike for sale is not for young children.

B The bike is not very good anymore.

C James is selling the bike because he doesn't like the colour.

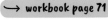

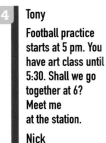

4 Tony
Football practice starts at 5 pm. You have art class until 5:30. Shall we go together at 6? Meet me at the station.
Nick

A Nick knows Tony can't be at football practice when it starts.

B Nick wants to go to football practice a bit earlier than Tony.

C Nick wants to be with Tony, but doesn't want to go to football practice.

Hi Karen
The Blue Tomatoes are playing in Hyde Park next Sunday. I'm going. The tickets are not cheap, but they're great! Come with me!
Sarah

A Sarah has got tickets for her and for Karen.

B Sarah hopes that Karen comes with her.

C Sarah hopes that Karen pays for her ticket.

5
Baking sale
Strawberry cakes
Buy one, get one free!
(Special offer 3–6 pm only!)

A The cake shop is only open after 3 pm.

B You can only get strawberry cakes from 3 to 6.

C Two cakes will cost the same as one.

Brighton Zoo
Half-price tickets this weekend:
groups of 10 or more
Book online only

A You can get a discount on tickets by booking online or at the zoo.

B If you visit the zoo alone, tickets are more expensive.

C Only groups of ten or more can book zoo tickets this weekend.

6 Liz
Sorry you're ill. Don't forget the story writing competition. Miss Smith says we have to complete it by next Monday.
Love, Anne

Anne wrote this message

A to check if Liz finished her story.

B to let Liz know what they did in class today.

C to tell her about something she needs to do.

LISTENING
Part 4: 3-option multiple choice

→ **workbook page 79**

2 🔊 **8.07** **For each question, choose the correct answer.**

1 You will hear a man talking to his son. What does the man want his son to do?
A Finish his homework quickly.
B Help him in the garden.
C Work more carefully.

2 You will hear a girl, Kate, talking about shopping. Why did she buy the camera?
A The colour was right.
B The size was right.
C The price was right.

3 You will hear a woman talking to her daughter. What's the weather like?
A It's windy.
B It's wet.
C It's cold.

4 You will hear a teacher talking to her student, Sebastian. What is he going to do after school?
A He's going to see the doctor.
B He's going to help his parents.
C He's going to visit his mother.

5 You will hear two friends talking about their day. What did they do?
A They went to an adventure park.
B They went cycling.
C They went running.

TEST YOURSELF

 VOCABULARY

1 **Complete the sentences with the words in the list. There are two extra words.**

> basketball | calculator | does | hair dryer | headphones | make
> remote control | skiing | sailing | satnav | up | windsurfing

1 We're lost. We need a _____ .
2 I have to _____ my bed every morning before I go to school.
3 The kitchen's a mess. Someone should do the washing-_____ .
4 I love _____ . I've got a small boat and I go every weekend.
5 What is 319 divided by 11? That's hard. I need a _____ .
6 I was playing _____ when the ball hit me on the head.
7 I want to watch the news. Pass me the _____ , please.
8 My mum was _____ and she fell over in the snow three times!
9 Dad _____ the cooking in my house.
10 I'm trying to work and your music is too loud. Use your _____ , please.

/10

Ⓖ GRAMMAR

2 **Complete the sentences with the past simple or past continuous form of the verbs.**

> eat | find | see | stop | walk | watch

1 She _____ in the park when I saw her.
2 I was tidying my room when I _____ my favourite pen that I lost last week.
3 The docking station _____ working while we were listening to music.
4 We started running when we _____ the bus.
5 I _____ my dinner when the phone rang.
6 We _____ TV when Mum called us for dinner.

3 **Find and correct the mistake in each sentence.**

1 My mum and dad was playing in the garden with my brother.
2 You not have to go if you don't want to.
3 We mustn't run. The bus doesn't go for an hour.
4 You must to be careful. It's very dangerous.
5 She played football when she broke her leg.
6 Yesterday the sports shop was sell them for only £15.

/12

⚙ FUNCTIONAL LANGUAGE

4 **Write the missing words.**

1 **A** You _____ have to watch the film it if you don't want to.
  B Thanks, I don't _____ like it.
2 **A** I can't come out tonight. I've got lots of things to do.
  B Like _____ ?
  A Well, I've got to help my dad _____ the shopping, for a start.
3 **A** At _____ , I was a bit scared, but _____ a while I was OK.
4 **A** What _____ you doing at nine o'clock?
  B I was _____ the washing-up.

/8

MY SCORE /30
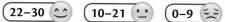
22–30 😊 10–21 😐 0–9 😟

83

9 WILD AND WONDERFUL

OBJECTIVES

FUNCTIONS:
talking about the weather; paying compliments

GRAMMAR:
comparative adjectives; *can / can't* for ability; superlative adjectives

VOCABULARY:
geographical features; the weather; phrases with *with*

Get TH!NKING

▶25

Watch the video and think: what natural wonders do you see every day?

📖 READING

1 **Look at the photos. Which of the animals can you name in English?**

2 **Name other animals in English. Write them down.**

3 SPEAKING **Work in pairs. Look at the animals on your list. What countries do you think of?**

> *Lions come from South Africa.*

> *You find horses all over the world.*

4 SPEAKING **Work in pairs. Look at the photos again and answer the questions.**

1 Do these animals live in hot or cold places?
2 What do you think they eat?
3 What dangers are there where they live?
4 What is the relationship between these animals and people?
5 Do people hunt these animals? Why or why not?
6 What is interesting about these places for tourists?

5 🔊 9.01 **Read and listen to the article. Mark the statements T (true) or F (false). Correct the false information.**

1 More than half the people in the world live in cities.
2 When it rains in the Kalahari, the grass and the bushes turn from brown to green.
3 The Chimbu skeleton dancers are the only tribe living near Mt Wilhelm.
4 They paint skeletons on their bodies to scare away wild animals.
5 The Nenets always go where the reindeer are.
6 Young Kazakhs have to be strong to become golden eagle hunters.

6 SPEAKING **Work in pairs or small groups. Think about and answer these questions.**

1 Would you like to go to the places in the article? Why (not)?
2 Are you interested in the lives of people living in wild places? Why (not)?

> *I'd love to / I wouldn't like to ... because ...*

> *I'm (not) interested in ...*

> *I think it's too dangerous to ... / wonderful to ...*

> *I love / hate reading about ... watching documentaries about ...*

THE WILD
side of life

More and more people think that life is better in the city than the countryside. For the first time in history more than 50% of the world's population lives in urban areas. However, there are still many groups of people who live in some of the wildest places on the planet.

The Kalahari is a large area of bush land in southern Africa. It has two parts. The south part is drier than the north and plants do not grow there very well. Every year at the end of summer it rains and the land becomes more beautiful than at other times of the year. But the grass and the bushes soon get dry and turn brown again. Life there is difficult.

The San are a group of people who live in the Kalahari. They live in huts, eat wild animals – even lions – plants and berries. They are very good with bows and arrows, and use them for hunting.

Up in the mountains of central Papua New Guinea is the Chimbu Province. This jungle area is one of the world's most remote places. It is also home to Mt Wilhelm, the highest mountain on the island. Several different tribes live in the valleys between the mountains. One of these is the Chimbu skeleton dancers. They paint skeletons onto their bodies. This makes them look scarier and it frightens other people away from their land.

The Yamal Peninsula in northern Siberia is one and a half times bigger than France. It is frozen for much of the year and temperatures can reach -50°C in the winter. But this area is home to a tribe of about 10,000 people called the Nenets. The Nenets are nomadic, meaning they frequently move from one place to another. Each year around 300,000 reindeer move around the land and the Nenets always go with them. The recent discovery of gas in the area means more people than before are visiting the Yamal. So the Nenets now have more contact with the outside world.

The Bayan-Ölgii Province is the highest part of Mongolia. It is a wild area with many mountains, lakes, forests and rivers. It is also home to the Kazakh golden eagle hunters. These people travel around the mountains and use eagles to hunt for foxes and other small animals. When boys turn 13, they can become golden eagle hunters. However, they have to be stronger than most boys their age because they have to show that they can carry the weight of an eagle. There are about 100,000 Kazakh people, but only around 250 of them are golden eagle hunters.

TH!NK values

Valuing our world

7 Read and tick (✓) the statements that show that the natural world is important.

1 Why should I be interested in people living in wild places? There's nothing to learn from them. ☐

2 I want to organise trips to Papua New Guinea. People will pay a lot of money to see the skeleton dancers. ☐

3 It's great to learn about nature. It helps me to understand more about the world. ☐

4 Who needs wild animals? They're dangerous – and that's all! ☐

5 I watch a lot of nature programmes on TV. I support a project to save the tiger in India. ☐

8 SPEAKING Compare your ideas in pairs.

Statement 1 shows that the person does not know how wonderful our world is.

Why do you think that?

Because the person isn't interested in people living in wild places.

Maybe this person needs more information to understand how wonderful these places are.

GRAMMAR
Comparative adjectives

1 Look at the article on page 85. Find examples of comparisons. Then complete the table on the right.

2 Complete the sentences. Use the comparative form of the adjectives.

1 Africa is _____ (big) than Europe, but _____ (small) than Asia.

2 Be careful with the spiders in the Kalahari. They're _____ (dangerous) than in Europe.

3 Cars these days are _____ (good) quality than they were 30 years ago.

4 Sarah loves wildlife. For her, holidays in the Kalahari are _____ (interesting) than going to the seaside.

5 My sister has got two children. Her son is nine. His sister is two years _____ (young).

6 John is a musician. It's _____ (easy) for him to learn a new instrument than it is for me.

	adjectives	comparative form
short adjectives (one syllable)	small hot big	⁰*smaller* (than) hotter (than) ¹ _____ (than)
adjectives ending in consonant + -y	happy dry early	happier (than) ² _____ (than) earlier (than)
longer adjectives (two or more syllables)	attractive beautiful	more attractive (than) ³ _____ (than)
irregular adjectives	bad good far	worse (than) ⁴ _____ (than) farther / further (than)

→ workbook page 82

VOCABULARY
Geographical features

3 🔊 9.02 Label the picture with the words. Write 1–12 in the boxes. Then listen and check.

1 beach | **2** desert | **3** forest | **4** hill | **5** island | **6** jungle | **7** lake | **8** mountain | **9** ocean | **10** river

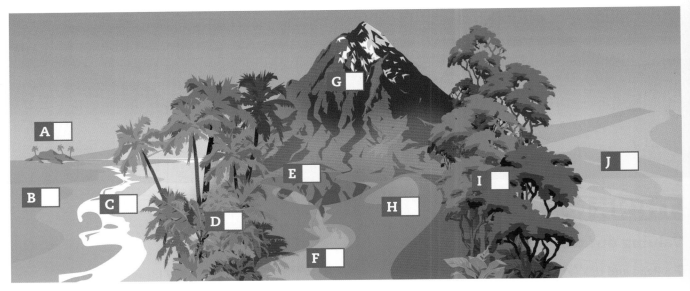

4 SPEAKING Work in pairs. Ask your partner to close their book and then ask them about the picture.

What's A?

I think it's … / I'm not sure if I can remember. Is it … ? / Can you give me the first letter, please?

5 SPEAKING Work in pairs. Compare some of the places. Use the adjectives in the list to help you, or use other adjectives.

beautiful | big | dangerous | difficult
exciting | high | hot | nice

A mountain is higher than a hill.

Yes, and it's more difficult to climb a mountain.

→ workbook page 84

🎧 LISTENING

6 Match the words in the list with the photos.
Write 1–4 in the boxes.

> **1** vultures | **2** a lion and its kill
> **3** a spear | **4** antelopes

 A

 C

 B

 D

7 🔊 9.03 Listen to an interview with a Kalahari bushman. Which title best summarises the interview?

1 Life in the Kalahari
2 Lions, vultures and antelopes
3 A young man's difficult task
4 Big cats can't run fast

8 🔊 9.03 Listen again. For questions 1–5, tick (✓) A, B or C.

1 Where was PK born?
   A in the Kalahari ☐
   B in the Sahara ☐
   C in Kenya ☐

2 Before a young man can get married, he has to
   A do a task. ☐
   B find a lion. ☐
   C kill an antelope. ☐

3 It's important for the future family that the young man
   A kills many lions. ☐
   B likes the girl's father. ☐
   C has courage. ☐

4 What can show the bushman where the lion is eating?
   A antelopes ☐
   B vultures ☐
   C his future family ☐

5 To take the kill away from the lion, you have to
   A run faster than the lion can. ☐
   B attack the lion with your spear. ☐
   C be very quiet and surprise the lion. ☐

 Grammar rap! ▶26

🇬 GRAMMAR
can / can't for ability

9 Complete the sentences with *can* or *can't*.

1 How _____ you find a lion and its kill?
2 You _____ get the kill from the lion at night.
3 How _____ you get the meat away from the lion?

10 Complete the table.

Positive	I/you/we/they/he/she/it **can** run fast.
Negative	I/you/we/they/he/she/it ¹_____ (**cannot**) run fast.
Questions	²_____ I/you/we/they/he/she/it run fast?
Short answers	Yes, I/you/we/they/he/she/it **can**. No, I/you/we/they/he/she/it ³_____ (**cannot**).

11 Make sentences with *can* and *can't*.

0 Simon + run fast / – swim fast
   Simon can run fast, but he can't swim fast.
1 Matt + drive a car / – fly a plane
   Matt _____
2 I + write emails / – do Maths on my laptop
   I _____
3 They + write stories / – spell well
   They _____

→ workbook page 82

WordWise: Phrases with *with*

12 Match the parts of the sentences.

1 They are very good ☐
2 The Nenets always go ☐
3 The Nenets now have more contact ☐
4 It's a wild area ☐

a with the reindeer.
b with bows and arrows.
c with many mountains.
d with the outside world.

13 Put the words in the correct order.

1 friend / with / came / My / me / best
2 not / I'm / very / computers / with / good
3 with / very / I'm / homework / my / busy

→ workbook page 84

READING

1 🔊 9.04 **Read and listen to the blog. Where was the biggest snowfall ever in one day? How much snow fell on that day?**

E✗TREME NATURE!

At 7.30 am on 22 January 1943, the people of Spearfish in South Dakota, US woke up to find the temperature outside was a freezing -20°C. Two minutes later, thermometers were showing a much warmer 7°C – a rise of 27°C in 120 seconds. But it didn't stop there. The temperature continued to go up and by 9 am it was 12°C. Just as the people started to think about enjoying a warm winter's day, the temperature fell 16°C in just under half an hour back down to -4°C and the residents had to put their coats back on! It was the most dramatic temperature change in the history of American weather.

The village of Capracotta is in the mountains near the Adriatic coast of Italy. It gets a lot of snow in the winter. But on 5 March 2015 its 1,000 inhabitants saw 256 cm of snowfall in 18 hours. It was the biggest snowfall ever in a day. One photo taken on the day shows a woman in a house shaking hands through the window with her neighbour in the street. The neighbour is standing on top of the snow. The woman is on the second floor of her home!

Do you like long sunny days? Then the best city in the world to live in is Reykjavik. 21 June is the longest day of the year in the northern hemisphere and the Icelandic capital gets 21 hours and 45 minutes of daylight. The sun hardly ever goes down. However, Reykjavik could also be the worst place to be. On the shortest day of the year, 21 December, the sun hardly rises there and people get only four hours and seven minutes of daylight. But during winter nights, you can often see the Northern Lights – one of the world's most beautiful natural events.

2 **Read the blog again. Answer the questions.**

1 How quickly did the temperature change from 12°C to -4°C in Spearfish?

2 What happened in Capracotta on 5 March 2015?

3 What makes the long winter nights in Reykjavik better?

 SPEAKING

3 **Work in pairs. Discuss these questions.**

1 Which of the facts did you know before?

2 Which of the facts were new to you?

3 Which of the places mentioned would you like to visit most? Why?

4 **Can you think of an amazing weather event in your country? Use the questions below to help you.**

Did a lot of snow fall?

Did it rain heavily or was there a very strong wind?

Was it very hot or was it very cold?

Where were you that day? What did you do? How did you feel?

PRONUNCIATION

Vowel sounds: /ɪ/ and /aɪ/ Go to page 121. 🎧

 WRITING

An email about an amazing weather event

5 **Imagine you want to tell a friend about an amazing weather event. Write an email (100–125 words).**

• Choose the place.

• In your email, say:

  – where the place is

  – what was special about the weather and when it happened

  – how the people reacted

Ⓖ **GRAMMAR**

Superlative adjectives

6 **Put the words in order to make sentences. Check your answers in the article.**

1 temperature change / the / of / was / the / American weather / It / in / most dramatic / history

2 day / snowfall / the biggest / was / ever / It / a / in

3 is / day of the year / 21 June / longest / the / in / hemisphere / the / northern

4 worst / be / Reykjavik / to / However / be / also / the / could / place

7 Look at the table. Complete the 'adjectives' column with the words in the list. Then complete the comparative and superlative forms.

bad | beautiful | happy | hot | ~~warm~~

	adjectives	comparative form	superlative form
short adjectives (one syllable)	0 _____warm_____	warmer	the warmest
	short	5 _____	14 _____
	long	6 _____	15 _____
short adjectives ending in one vowel + one consonant	1 _____	hotter	16 _____
	big	7 _____	17 _____
adjectives ending in consonant + -y	sunny	8 _____	18 _____
	2 _____	happier	19 _____
longer adjectives (two or more syllables)	3 _____	more beautiful	the most beautiful
	difficult	9 _____	20 _____
	dramatic	10 _____	21 _____
irregular adjectives	4 _____	11 _____	the worst
	good	12 _____	22 _____
	far	13 _____	23 _____

8 Complete the sentences. Use the superlative form of the adjectives.

0 It's Cindy's birthday tomorrow. She's _____the happiest_____ (happy) girl in class.

1 Brazil is _____ (big) country in South America.

2 I had an awful headache this morning. I think I did _____ (bad) test ever.

3 I think social media is _____ (good) way of contacting people.

4 She's great at Maths. She can solve _____ (difficult) sums.

→ workbook page 83

VOCABULARY
The weather

9 🔊 9.07 Write the words under the pictures. Listen and check.

cloudy | cold | dry | foggy | freezing | hot | humid | rainy | sunny | warm | wet | windy

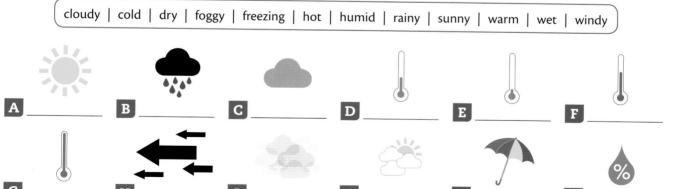

A _____ B _____ C _____ D _____ E _____ F _____

G _____ H _____ I _____ J _____ K _____ L _____

10 Think about the different kinds of weather. Write reasons why you think they can be good.

a sunny day: We can ride our bikes.
a hot day: We can go swimming.
a rainy day: We can play computer games.

11 SPEAKING Work in pairs. Make dialogues about the weather with a partner.

What a nice day.

Yes, it's really warm. Let's ride our bikes.

Great idea.

→ workbook page 84

1 🔊 9.08 **Look at the photo. What do you think is happening? Why? Listen and read to check.**

James: Excuse me. Can we get our ball, please?

Alice: Yes, of course.

James: Oh, what a lovely garden!

Alice: Thank you. That's a nice thing to say. Do you like gardening, then?

James: Well, not really. I don't know much about flowers and things. But my sister loves them, don't you, Gill?

Gill: That's right. And your flowers really look wonderful. I love your roses.

Alice: Thank you again. I do it all myself, you know. My husband helped me before, but he can't walk very well now, so I have to do it all. It's a lot of work. I get very, very tired.

Gill: Well, we can help you – can't we, James?

James: We're in the middle of a game and I'm winning! Maybe another day.

Gill: We can finish our game later, James. What would you like us to do?

Alice: What nice people you are! Well, perhaps you can help me move the table and chairs under that tree. They're in the sun at the moment and it's very hot. But first, I just need to make a phone call and a cup of tea. I'll be back in a minute.

James: No problem. We're fine here. OK. Let's move the table first. We can do that together. Then the chairs.

moments later …

Alice: Oh, that's fantastic. Well done! Look, let me give you some money for some ice cream or chocolate. To say thank you.

Gill: No, please. We're happy to help. Come on, James. Bye!

James: How nice! She wanted to give us some money!

Gill: I know. And I feel so good now. I don't want ice cream, or chocolate, either. Her smile was enough.

James: That's right. But let's get some ice cream anyway!

2 🔊 9.08 **Read and listen again and answer the questions.**

1 What does James say about Alice's garden?
2 Why does Alice's husband not help her?
3 What does Alice ask them to do?
4 Why does Alice want to give them money?
5 Why does Gill say 'no' to Alice's money?

3 **Imagine you were in James and Gill's situation. Would you take the money that Alice wants to give them? Why (not)?**

Phrases for fluency

4 **Find the expressions 1–5 in the dialogue. Who says them? How do you say them in your language?**

0 … in a minute. *Alice*   3 No problem. _____
1 Well done! _____   4 … , not really. _____
2 … , either. _____   5 … , then? _____

5 **Complete the conversations with the expressions in Exercise 4.**

1 **A** I got 97% in the test, Dad.
  B _____ ! Did you study hard for it, _____ ?
2 **A** Hi, David. I can't talk right now. Sorry. I'll phone you _____ , OK?
  B _____ , Chris. Call me back when you can.
3 **A** Did you enjoy the film?
  B No, _____ . I didn't like the book very much, _____ .

⚙️ FUNCTIONS
Paying compliments

KEY LANGUAGE
What a lovely … !   … really looks wonderful.   I love …

6 **Use the words from the Key Language box to write compliments.**

1 Your friend is wearing a new jacket that you think is lovely.
  You: _____ !
2 Your friend is drawing a very nice picture. You really like it.
  You: _____ .
3 Your friend has got a new hairstyle and you really like it.
  You: _____ !

7 **Work in pairs. Use the photos to make compliments.**

What a lovely voice!

LIFE COMPETENCIES

We all belong to communities – our family, our school, our town, our country – and there is always something everybody thinks should be better for that community. It's easy to do nothing and wait for other people to help. Helping our community isn't always easy, but it feels good.

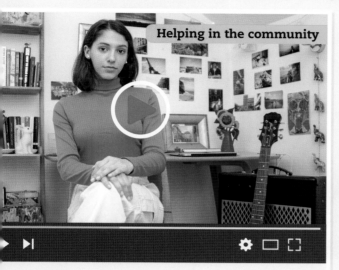

Helping in the community

1 ▶ 27 **Watch the video. How many neighbours does she talk about? How does she help her community?**

2 ▶ 27 **Watch again and answer the questions.**

1 Who gives her the project?

2 How does she feel when he gets the project?

3 What is the project?

4 What does she learn about:

*   a Mr Rodgers?*

*   b Mrs Thomas?*

*   c Mr Saunders?*

5 How does she feel about the

*   project now?*

3 Read about the Under the Tree Foundation. What does it do?

4 Work in pairs. Choose a community. Write all the difficulties you can think of for people in that community. Use the examples to help you.

Your country – homeless people …

The world – places with no clean water …

Your town/local area – rubbish on the streets …

Your school – books in your classroom need organising …

Your family – the car is dirty …

5 Exchange and share your ideas with another pair who wrote about a different community. Then write ideas on ways your class can help with these problems.

Me and my world

6 SPEAKING **Tick (✓) the sentences that are true for you. Compare with a partner.**

- [ ] I know most of the people where I live.
- [ ] I talk to my neighbours almost every day.
- [ ] There is a good community spirit where I live.
- [ ] I sometimes help with local projects.
- [ ] I'd like to be more involved in my local community.
- [ ] A happy community is good for everyone.

TIPS FOR HELPING IN THE COMMUNITY

- Identify what you are not happy about in your community and think of ways of improving it.
- Always put the objectives of the community above your personal goals.
- Don't be afraid to offer your own suggestions, but listen and consider the opinions of others.

When he was 12, Jonathan Woods went Christmas shopping and had a great idea. He was buying toys to give to an organisation in his town. They gave the toys to young children whose parents didn't have enough money to buy Christmas presents. While he was looking for presents to buy, he had a thought. The organisation helped young children, but many older children his age were probably in the same situation as the young children. Who was buying presents for them?

Jonathan decided to start an organisation to buy Christmas presents for older children. He called it the Under the Tree Foundation. He also asked an organisation working with older children and teenagers in his local area for advice on what to buy.

In 2007, Jonathan sent letters to all his friends and family asking them to help Under the Tree. The response to these letters was fantastic. Twenty-five older children received the presents they'd wanted for Christmas, and over 80 teenagers were invited to a pizza and movie night.

The next year, Under the Tree bought presents for over 50 children. The organisation still continues to help older children have a better Christmas.

10 OUT AND ABOUT

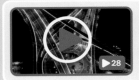

Get **TH!NK**ING

Watch the video and think: what is unique about your town?

▶28

A

C

B

D

 READING

1 **Look at the photos. In which one can you see these things? Where are the places?**

1 a very famous **statue**
2 a **sports stadium**
3 a really long **wall**
4 a **park** in a city centre

2 SPEAKING **Work in pairs. Name more places you can find in a town.**

museum, shop, station

3 SPEAKING **How important are these places for a town? Think about who each place is important for and why. Compare your ideas with another pair.**

4 **Work in pairs. Discuss the questions.**

1 What interesting places for tourists are there in your town or city?
2 What interesting events for tourists are there?

5 ◁)) 10.01 **Read and listen to the emails. Answer the questions.**

1 Where are the writers writing from?
2 What do they think of the places?
3 What is different about the two people writing these emails?

6 ◁)) 10.01 **Read and listen to the emails again and mark the sentences A (true), B (false) or C (doesn't say).**

1 Ryan had problems with his flight.
   A True   B False   C Doesn't say
2 Ryan is in a band and they are going to play in a famous concert hall.
   A True   B False   C Doesn't say
3 Ryan's band is the only one from Europe.
   A True   B False   C Doesn't say
4 Bettina and her team lost the match against the under-15 Beijing champions.
   A True   B False   C Doesn't say
5 Bettina would like to see the Great Wall, but she can't because she has to go back to Beijing.
   A True   B False   C Doesn't say
6 She cannot play volleyball for six weeks.
   A True   B False   C Doesn't say

Mum
Mrs_hudson@thinkmail.com

Hi Mum!!

Hi Mum,

It's Day Two and I'm already in love with New York. It's amazing. The first day, we were pretty tired from the flight, but we did a bit of sightseeing in the afternoon. We went to see the Statue of Liberty and I wasn't disappointed. We had a guided tour and learned all about its history. It really is a powerful symbol of peace.

Today, we're going to explore Central Park and Manhattan. In the evening, we're going to watch the New York Jets. They're playing at MetLife Stadium. It's my first game of American football and I'm looking forward to it. (I think – I'm quite nervous!)

The big concert we're playing in is tomorrow and we're all getting quite excited. Just imagine, I'm going to play my trombone in Carnegie Hall, probably the most famous concert hall in the US. Mr Davis is even more excited. He's going to conduct us in the concert. He keeps telling us it's his dream come true. His wife's going to record the performance. She's going to send us all the link so you can see the greatest moment of my musical career so far! There are going to be bands from all over the world, from about 20 different countries. I can't wait!

Hope you're well and not missing me too much!

Love,

Ryan

Abigail
abi@mymail.com

China!

Hi Abigail,

Sorry I didn't write yesterday, but it was such a busy day I just didn't get the time. We played our second volleyball match of the trip. It was against the under-15 Beijing champions and they won easily. I also hurt my hand quite badly. The sports centre where we played was fantastic. Really modern and much better than ours back home. Anyway, I've got ten minutes to write to you quickly, then I'm going to the bus station to catch a bus to Luanping. I'm so excited because we're going to visit the Great Wall. It was probably the one thing I wanted to do most on this trip, after playing volleyball, of course! 😊 We're going to explore the Jinshanling section of the wall. It's in the mountains and it's quite a walk to get up to it. But the views are spectacular. I'm going to take loads of photos. Luanping is about 130 km away, so we're going to spend the night there. Then we're going back to Beijing for our last day in the city. Our last match is in the afternoon, but I'm not going to play because of my hand. I can't believe the trip is almost over. China is amazing and the Chinese people are so friendly. I want to stay longer.

Lots of love,

Bettina

TH!NK values

Appreciating other cultures

7 **Read and tick (✓) the things you do.**

You are on an exchange trip in a new country for two weeks. Which of these things would you do?

☐ Make friends with the local children.

☐ Try and find children from your own country who are also on holiday there.

☐ Try and learn some of the local language.

☐ Speak your own language (and hope people understand you).

☐ See if the TV has programmes from your own country.

☐ Read the books you brought from home.

☐ Visit the museums.

☐ Listen to and buy some music by musicians from that country.

8 **SPEAKING** **Work in pairs. Decide which of the things in Exercise 7 are good to help you find out more about a different culture. What other things can you think of that are also good to do?**

Grammar rap!

▶29

GRAMMAR
be going to for intentions

1 Complete the sentences from the emails on page 93 with the correct form of *be*. Then complete the rule.

0 I _'m___ going to take loads of photos.
1 Today, we _____ going to explore Central Park.
2 His wife _____ going to record the performance.
3 There _____ going to be bands from all over the world.
4 We _____ going to visit the Great Wall.

> **RULE:** We use *be going to* to talk about our intentions for the ⁵*future* / *present*. Use the present tense of *be* + *going to* + ⁶*base form* / *-ing form* of the verb.

2 Complete the table.

Positive	Negative	Questions	Short answers
I'm (am) going to play.	I'm not (am not) going to play.	Am I going to play?	Yes, ⁵_____ . No, I'm not.
You/we/they're (are) going to play.	You/we/they ¹_____ (are not) going to play.	³_____ you/we/they going to play?	Yes, you/we/they ⁶_____ . No, you/we/they aren't.
He/she/it's (is) going to play.	He/she/it ²_____ (is not) going to play.	⁴_____ he/she/it going to play?	Yes, he/she/it is. No, he/she/it ⁷_____ .

3 Complete the future intentions with the correct form of the verbs.

> ~~not watch~~ | take | not fight | not borrow | eat

0 I _I'm not going to watch___ so much TV.
1 My parents _____ out more often.
2 My brother _____ with me anymore.
3 I _____ the dog for a walk every day.
4 My sisters _____ my clothes without asking anymore.

4 Look at the table. Tick (✓) the things you are going to do.

tonight	this week	this year
do homework	play sport	write a blog
watch TV	visit relatives	have a holiday
tidy your room	play a computer game	learn something new

5 **SPEAKING** Ask and answer questions about the activities above.

Are you going to watch TV tonight? *Yes, I am.* ⟶ **workbook page 90**

VOCABULARY
Places in town

6 Match the places in the town with the people. Write 1–8 in the boxes.

> 1 concert hall | 2 sports centre
> 3 shopping mall | 4 bus station
> 5 police station | 6 post office
> 7 football stadium | 8 car park

7 **SPEAKING** Work in pairs. Describe a place from Exercise 6 for your partner to guess.

You go here to buy clothes.

⟶ **workbook page 92**

A ☐   E ☐

B ☐   F ☐

C ☐   G ☐

D ☐   H ☐

LISTENING

8 🔊 **10.02** Listen to Olivia and Connor. When is the History test?

9 🔊 **10.02** Listen again and mark the statements T (true) or F (false).

1 Connor has an important football match on Saturday.
2 Connor is celebrating his birthday at an American restaurant.
3 Olivia is not a fan of superhero films.
4 Connor invites Olivia to the museum.
5 Connor has about an hour between getting back from the museum and his piano lesson.
6 Connor isn't very busy the following weekend.

G GRAMMAR
Present continuous for arrangements

10 Look at the examples. Choose the correct options.

1 What *are you doing / do you do* this weekend?
2 Dad's *taking / takes* me to the sports centre. We're *going to watch / watch* the basketball game.

11 Complete the rule with the words in the list.

present | future | arrangements

RULE: We can use the ¹_____ continuous to talk about ²_____ for the ³_____ .

12 Complete the sentences. Use the present continuous form of the verb.

0 I ____*'m going*____ (go) to Dan's party on Saturday.
1 Oliver _____ (not come) to my house this afternoon.
2 Jessica and I _____ (do) our homework together after school.
3 We _____ (not visit) my grandparents on Sunday.
4 _____ your class _____ (go) on a trip next week?
5 My brother _____ (play) in the basketball final on Monday.

13 Complete the conversation. Use the present continuous form of the verbs in the list.

not do (x2) | go | buy | meet | do (x2) | play

Kenny   What ¹_____ you _____ this afternoon?
Elena   Nothing. I ²_____ anything.
Kenny   Paul and I ³_____ football. Do you want to come?
Elena   OK. Can I invite Tim? He ⁴_____ anything, either.
Kenny   Sure. And what about your brother? ⁵_____ he _____ anything?
Elena   Yes, he ⁶_____ shopping with my mum. They ⁷_____ his birthday present.
Kenny   OK. Well, we ⁸_____ Jack, Adam, Lucy and Julia at the park at two.
Elena   OK. See you at two, then.

→ *workbook page 90*

⚙ FUNCTIONS
Inviting and making arrangements

14 Put the words in order to make sentences. Which sentences are accepting an invitation? Which ones are refusing?

1 like / with / you / Would / to / come / us
2 love / to / I'd
3 study / Do / want / together/ to / you
4 sorry / I'm / can't / I
5 great / That / be / would

15 Complete the exchanges.

1 A Would _____ go to the cinema with me?
  B _____ great.
2 A I'm going to the shops. Do _____ come with me?
  B I'm sorry. I _____ . I've got a lot to do.
3 A _____ like _____ meet up on Sunday?
  B Sunday? Yes. I _____ to.

16 Think of three arrangements and write them in your diary.

17 Can you complete your diary? Walk around the classroom and:

1 invite people to do things with you.
2 find things to do when you're free.

A

B

C

Home   About   Latest posts

As you probably know, the town council have got £1 million to spend on improving the town's facilities for young people and we're looking for great ideas on how to spend the money well. Post your ideas in the forum below and let us know how we can make life better for you.

1 There's nothing for teenagers to do in this town, especially at night. Can we use the money to build a youth club? Somewhere with a pool table and a table tennis table, perhaps. We need somewhere to play happily and hang out safely in the evenings. *Daisy, 15*

2 As I'm only 14, I can't drive, so I go everywhere on my bike. But the roads are dangerous and many motorists drive too fast. How about spending the money on building more cycle lanes? We could also put in more speed cameras and zebra crossings, too. This will make life safer for all our citizens, not just the young people. *Liz, 14*

3 I think the best use for the money is to build a playground in the town park. It should have lots of rides for the young kids but also stuff for teenagers, too. I'd like to see a graffiti wall and a skateboard park for a start and maybe if there is enough money, we can have a climbing wall, too. *Luke, 13*

4 Our high street is full of empty shops because everyone just shops at the new shopping centre outside of town or online. Why don't we use the money to turn some of these empty shops into an arts centre? It can have studios where we can draw and paint or learn how to make films. We could also have a music studio where local bands can record music cheaply. *Alex, 17*

5 How about a big billboard at the entrance to the town that reads, 'TEEN WARNING – there's nothing to do here!' *Sadie, 16*

6 This probably sounds like a boring idea, but can't we use some of the money to buy more litter bins? I feel ashamed of our town when I see all the litter on the ground. We need to tidy up our town quickly! *Jack, 15*

D

E

F

READING

1 **Look at the photos. Which of them show problems? What are the problems?**

2 🔊 10.03 **Read and listen to the forum. Match the texts with the photos.**

3 **Read the entries again. Answer the questions.**
1 Why are these young people writing on the forum?
2 What does Daisy think young people need in the town?
3 What does Liz think is missing?
4 Why are there so many empty buildings on the high street?
5 What does Jack think is a big problem in the town?

Train to TH!NK

Problem solving

4 **SPEAKING** **Work in pairs. Read and discuss the problem.**

The young people in your town aren't happy.
They say there is nothing to do.
Make a list of suggestions to help solve this problem.

have a music festival   *build a skateboard park*

5 **Think about your suggestions. What are the advantages and disadvantages of each one?**

Suggestions	😊	😔
music festival	*young people love music / fun*	*noisy / make a mess / expensive*

6 **SPEAKING** **Decide which suggestion you think is the best. Compare your ideas with the rest of the class.**

> We think a musical festival is the best idea because all young people love music. It's also a lot of fun.

GRAMMAR
Adverbs

7 **Look at the sentences from the website on page 96. Make a list of adjectives and adverbs.**

0 We're looking for great ideas on how to spend the money well. *Adjective: great Adverb: well*

1 We need somewhere to play happily and hang out safely in the evenings.

2 Many motorists drive too fast.

3 Our high street is full of empty shops.

4 We could also have a music studio where local bands can record music cheaply.

5 This probably sounds like a boring idea.

6 We need to tidy up our town quickly!

8 **Complete the rule.**

> **RULE:** To form adverbs:
> • add ¹_____ to regular adjectives (e.g., *quick* ➜ *quickly*).
> • delete the *-y* and add ²_____ to adjectives ending in consonant + *-y*. (e.g., *happy* ➜ *happily*).
> Some adjectives have irregular adverb forms.
> e.g., *fast* ➜ *fast*   *good* ➜ ³_____
> Adverbs usually come immediately after the object of the verb or the verb (if there is no object).
> *He plays tennis* **well**. NOT ~~*He plays well tennis*~~.

9 **Complete the sentences. Choose the correct words and write them in the correct form.**

0 His car was really __*fast*__ . He won the race __*easily*__ . (easy / fast)

1 It's not _____ . You need to do it very _____ . (careful / easy)

2 We need to walk _____ . I don't want to be _____ . (late / quick)

3 I did my homework _____ . I was really _____ . (tired / bad)

4 He drives really _____ . I get quite _____ in the car with him. (scared / dangerous)

➜ workbook page 91

VOCABULARY
Things in town: compound nouns

10 **Choose a word from A and a word from B to make things you can find in a town. Look at the website on page 96 to help you.**

> **A** bill | cycle | graffiti | high litter | ~~speed~~ | youth | zebra
> **B** bin | board | ~~camera~~ | club crossing | lane | street | wall

11 **Complete the sentences with the words in Exercise 10.**

0 Slow down. There's a _____*speed camera*_____ just ahead.

1 I really like that _____ advertising the new Italian restaurant has in town.

2 Don't drop your paper on the ground. There's a _____ behind you.

3 Don't try and cross the road here – there's a _____ just down there.

4 We live in a flat above one of the shops in the _____ .

5 The new _____ is really popular. Loads of people are painting on it.

6 I ride my bike to school. There's a _____ from outside my house all the way there.

7 We go to the _____ every Friday night. I usually play table tennis and chat with my friends there.

➜ workbook page 92

> **PRONUNCIATION**
> Voiced /ð/ and unvoiced /θ/ consonants
> Go to page 121. 🎧

TH!NK
Mythical places around the world
▶30

Culture

1 **Look at the pictures. What do you think a mythical place is?**

2 **Read the article quickly. Where are each of the places?**

3 🔊 **10.06** **Read the article again and listen. Mark the sentences T (true) or F (false).**

1 Many people have heard about Atlantis, but it is not very clear where and what it is.
2 The legend says that the people of Atlantis were famous for their culture and education.
3 Jules Verne knew where to find Agartha.
4 People believed that El Dorado was made of gold.
5 Plato was the first person to write about the island of Thule.
6 There is a story that Thule is a dark place, but a lot of great food grows there.

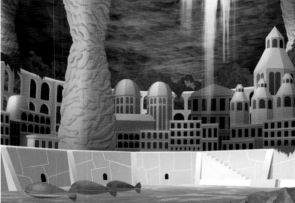

Mythical PLACES AROUND THE WORLD

There are very few places on Earth that are undiscovered and we have satellite photos of the most remote places on the planet. But people are always interested in mythical lands, places that people say exist but no one has ever found.

Perhaps the most famous mythical place of all is **Atlantis**. Some people say it is a city, others say it is an island and others call it a continent. But whatever it is exactly, there is one thing that everyone agrees on: it is underneath the sea. The Greek philosopher Plato was the first person to describe it and he suggested that one time, its people attacked Athens. No one is sure exactly where Atlantis is. Because of its name, some people think it is somewhere in the Atlantic Ocean. Others say it's in the Mediterranean Sea or in the Caribbean.

Agartha is another mythical place that is not on the land. The legend says that it's at the centre of our planet. Like Atlantis, it is famous for its culture and educated society. It was the inspiration for Jules Verne's novel *Journey to the Centre of the Earth*. It tells the story of a group of travellers who go on an exciting adventure underground. Many people have tried to find the entrance to Agartha, which they think is somewhere in Antarctica.

Some people believe that somewhere in South America there is a famous city of gold: **El Dorado**. Many people tried to find it, but they weren't successful. El Dorado was originally the name of a person, a ruler of the ancient Colombian society called the Muisca. He covered himself in gold powder every day. There were legends in which people imagined that the whole city was made of gold.

Our final mythical land is an island called **Thule**. The legend says that it is in the north of the Earth, somewhere between Norway and Iceland. This is an area of the world that is completely dark for a lot of the year. But the story goes that Thule is a place where a lot of delicious food grows and people are always happy. The Roman poet Silius Italicus wrote about Thule. In his story, the people living there are painted blue.

4  **VOCABULARY** **There are six highlighted words in the article. Match the words with these meanings. Write the words.**

0 not real, with lots of stories about it   *mythical*
1 a large group of people who live
   together in an organised way   _____
2 leader of a country or kingdom   _____
3 far away from people and places   _____
4 without light   _____
5 an old story   _____

5 **SPEAKING** **Work in pairs. Discuss.**

1 Imagine you are going to make a film set in one of these mythical places. Think about the following:
   • What kind of film is it? (horror, love, science fiction?)
   • What's the story about briefly? (It's about a …)
   • Who is going to star in your film? (It's going to star my favourite actors …)
2 Present your ideas to the group and vote on the best idea.

✏ WRITING
An informal email

1 **INPUT** **Read the email. Answer the questions.**

1 Where is Emily going to spend her summer holidays?
2 What is she going to do there?

2 **Find these expressions in the email. Use them to answer the questions below.**

> Guess what? | You won't believe it.
> I can't wait. | By the way, … | Anyway, …

1 Which two expressions do we use to change topic?
2 Which two expressions do we use to introduce some surprising news?
3 Which expression means 'I'm really excited'?

3 **ANALYSE** **Look at paragraphs 1 and 2 of Emily's email. Match the functions with the paragraphs. Write a–d.**

Paragraph 1: _____ and _____
Paragraph 2: _____ and _____

a Describe the city
b Give news
c Ask how your friend is
d Talk about your plans

4 **What is the function of paragraph 3?**

 Luke
luckyluke@writeme.co.uk

Exciting news!

Hi Luke,

[1] How are you? I hope you're not studying too hard. Don't worry, there are only two more weeks of school. Anyway, I'm writing because I've got some really cool news. You won't believe it. Mum and Dad are taking me to Cape Town for the summer. Cape Town, South Africa! I can't wait.

[2] So I did some research on the internet. It looks like a really amazing place. Of course, there's the famous Table Mountain and the waterfront markets, but there are so many other great things to do there. I'm definitely going to go on a safari. And guess what? Mum's going to buy me some hang-gliding lessons. I'm going to be a hang-glider! We're going to be there for the whole of August. It's winter there, but I think the South African winter is hotter than our summer. So that's it – my big news. What do you think?

[3] By the way, Dad says we're going to be in Newquay next weekend. Is there any chance we can meet up? Let me know.

Love,

Emily

5 **Which paragraph answers these questions?**

a What famous mountain is there in Cape Town?
b What's your news?
c How long are you going to stay in Cape Town?
d What's the weather like in Cape Town?
e What are you going to do in Cape Town?
f Where are you going?

6 **PRODUCE** **Imagine you are going to spend your next holiday in a famous city. Write an email (about 100–120 words) to your friend telling her the news.**

• Use the questions in Exercise 5 to help you.
• Use some of the language in Exercise 2.

A2 Key for Schools

📖 READING AND WRITING
Part 7: Picture story → *workbook page 61*

1 Look at the three pictures. Write the story shown in the pictures. Write 35 words or more.

Part 5: Open cloze

2 For each question, write the correct answer.

Write **one** word for each gap.

→ *workbook page 43*

My name ⁰ _*is*_ Hugo. I live in the north of Wales in a town called Llandudno. My
town has ¹_____ unusual name because it's Welsh. I ²_____ born here, so I speak Welsh really well.
I think Llandudno is ³_____ most beautiful town in Wales. It's by the sea and I love ⁴_____ go swimming.
In Llandudno, there ⁵_____ parks, a small mountain with a café at the top, and a really good concert hall where great bands play. Every Friday night I meet ⁶_____ my friends to play games and have some fun in Llandudno.

🎧 LISTENING
Part 2: Gap fill → *workbook page 79*

3 🔊 10.07 For each question, write the correct answer in the gap. Write one word or a number or a date or a time.

You will hear some information about a shopping centre. Listen and complete each question.

Blue Water
Shopping Centre

🧺 Number of shops: ⁰ _300_

🍴 Restaurants and a ¹_____ on fifth floor

🚗 Parking: £²_____ per hour

🚌 Buses to the city centre every ³_____ minutes

🏷 Shops open until 7.30 – every day except ⁴_____

👆 Website: ⁵_____

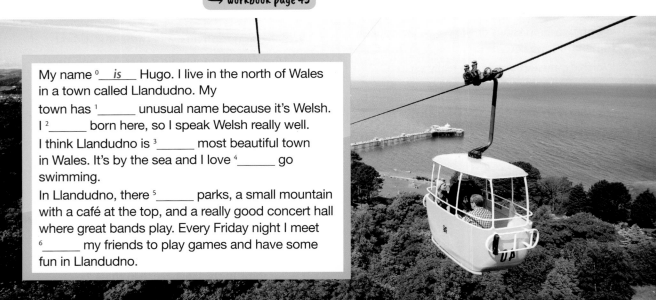

 VOCABULARY

1 Complete the sentences with the words in the list. There are two extra words.

> bin | cloudy | hall | house | island | lake | lanes | mountains | station | sunny | windy | zebra

1 It's very _____ today. You can't see the sun at all.
2 We live on a small _____ . We're always close to the sea.
3 Mum and Dad are going to the concert _____ tonight. They love classical music.
4 It's one of the highest _____ in the world and it took the climbers three days to get to the top.
5 It's so _____ that my hat just blew off my head.
6 Don't try and cross the road here. There's a _____ crossing just up there.
7 It's easy to get about town on a bike because there are cycle _____ everywhere.
8 Someone stole my bike last night. I went to the police _____ , but they say it's hard to find stolen bikes.
9 Put your rubbish in the litter _____ over there.
10 We went swimming in the _____ – the water was really cold!

          /10

GRAMMAR

2 Put the words in order to make sentences.

1 going / She's / nine / to / me / at / phone
2 Friday / We're / afternoon / on / leaving
3 homework / carefully / her / did / very / She
4 bag / I / remember / my / where / can't / left / I
5 the / It's / day / coldest / of / year / the
6 than / It's / mine / car / expensive / a / more

3 Find and correct the mistake in each sentence.

1 I speak badly Spanish.
2 He is the more popular footballer in the world; everybody likes him.
3 I had a lot of presents. But the one most I liked was a new bag from my mother.
4 She plays hockey very good.
5 He's ten and he still can't to ride a bike.
6 We are to meeting him at ten o'clock tomorrow.

          /12

FUNCTIONAL LANGUAGE

4 Write the missing words.

1 A _____ a wonderful day!
   B Yes, _____ go for a walk in the park.
2 A What are you _____ this afternoon?
   B Nothing. Why?
   A _____ you want to go skateboarding with me?
3 A _____ you like to come to my place for lunch on Saturday?
   B I'd _____ to. Thanks.
4 A _____ what?
   B What?
   A Mum's taking me to London next weekend. I _____ wait!

          /8

MY SCORE   /30

22–30   10–21   0–9

11 FUTURE BODIES

OBJECTIVES

FUNCTIONS:
making predictions; sympathising

GRAMMAR:
will / won't for future predictions; first conditional; time clauses with *when / as soon as*

VOCABULARY:
parts of the body; expressions with *do*; *when* and *if*

Get TH!NKING

Watch the video and think: how will life be in 100 years?

▶31

READING

1 **Label the picture with the words in the list. Write 1–12 in the boxes.**

> **1** arm | **2** bone | **3** ear | **4** eye | **5** finger
> **6** foot | **7** hair | **8** leg | **9** mouth
> **10** muscle | **11** thumb | **12** toe

2 **Write the words from Exercise 1 in the correct column. Some words can go in both columns.**

Body	Face
arm	mouth

3 **SPEAKING** **Work in pairs. Discuss the questions.**

Which parts of the body do you use when you:

- read a book?
- play football?
- watch television?
- make a phone call?
- eat a meal?
- walk to school?

> *When you read a book, you use your hands and your eyes.*

4 **Look at the picture and the title on page 103. What do you think the article will be about? Choose one of the following.**

- what we want to look like in the future
- what the human body will be like in the future
- how we can change our bodies if we want

5 🔊 11.01 **Read and listen to the article and check your ideas.**

6 **Read the article again and answer the questions.**

1 What is the most important reason why our bodies will change in the future?
2 Why will people be taller?
3 Why will people get weaker?
4 What will happen to eyes and fingers?
5 Why will we have one less toe?
6 Why won't people have so much hair on their bodies?

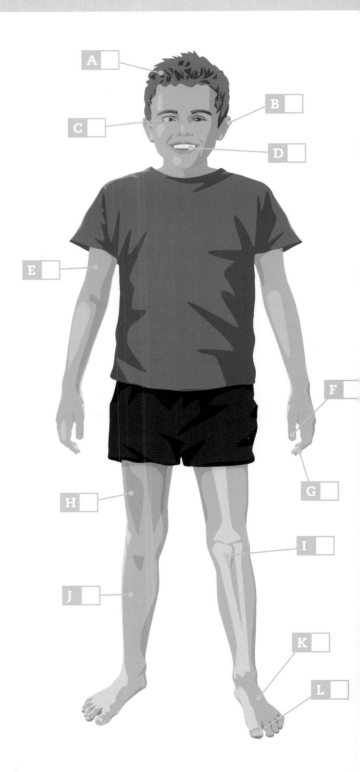

CHANGING BODIES

A long time ago, people were very different from the way we are now. For example, if you find a really old house somewhere, you'll see that the doors are usually much lower than they are today. Why? Because hundreds of years ago, people were shorter. Over time, the human body changes to adapt to a new way of life.

Can we expect the human body to change in the future? For sure. And the main reason is that we have more and more technology, and it is changing how we live.

What kind of changes can we expect? Well, no one can be 100 percent sure, but here are some possibilities.

1 Let's start with the example above. Humans are now ten centimetres taller than 150 years ago. So, in the future, people will probably be even taller. Most of us now have much better food than people in the past – and so we grow more.

2 We'll get weaker in more than one way. The most important way is that our muscles will not be as strong as now because we won't do a lot of physical work.

3 We are already using our feet less, and our hands more (think about computers and tablets and so on.) So we can expect that our legs will get shorter and our feet smaller, and at the same time, our fingers will get longer. And our fingers and our eyes will both get better because they'll have to do more work together.

4 Now, what about the mouth? It'll get smaller, perhaps, because technological improvements will mean that we don't need to talk so much – and also because our teeth will get smaller (so mouths don't need to be so big to keep them in).

5 Here's a good one – it's very possible that people will have four toes, not five. The little toe really isn't needed anymore (people who lose them don't miss them), so it will probably disappear sometime in the future.

6 And last but not least – people won't have as much hair on their bodies as now, as we don't need it to keep ourselves warm anymore.

Will all these things happen? And if so, when?
These are questions that no one can answer for sure.

TH!NK values

Exercise and health

7 Read the sentences. Give each one a number from 1 to 5 (1 = doesn't give a lot of importance to health, 5 = gives a lot of importance to health).

1. ☐ You should do regular exercise to make sure your muscles are strong.
2. ☐ It's OK to spend a lot of time sitting in front of the television.
3. ☐ A wonderful thing to do is go for long walks in the fresh air.
4. ☐ Using a computer and writing text messages gives your hands and arms exercise.
5. ☐ You don't have to do sport to be healthy and keep fit.
6. ☐ It's a good idea to do a lot of simple exercise (for example, use the stairs and don't take the lift).

8 SPEAKING Work in small groups. Talk about health and exercise.

1. Together, decide the number that the group is going to give to each of the sentences in Exercise 7.
2. Together, decide on and write another sentence that shows how the group feels about health and exercise.
3. Compare your ideas with other groups.

 **GRAMMAR**

will / won't for future predictions

1 Look at the sentences from the article on page 103. Complete with *will / 'll / will not / won't*. Then complete the rule.

1 Our fingers _____ get longer.
2 They _____ have to do more work together.
3 Our muscles _____ be as strong as now because we _____ do a lot of physical work.

> **RULE:** Use ⁴_____ (*will*) or ⁵_____ (*will not*) + base form of the verb to make predictions about the future.

2 Complete the table.

Positive	Negative
I/you/we/they/he/she/it ¹_____ (will) come.	I/you/we/they/he/she/it ²_____ (will not) come.

Questions	Short answers
³_____ I/you/we/they/he/she/it come?	Yes, I/you/we/they/he/she/it ⁴_____ . No, I/you/we/they/he/she/it ⁵_____ (will not).

3 Complete the conversation. Use *'ll, will* or *won't* and a verb from the list.

> be | get | give | go | help | see | stay

Alice Oh, Noah, it's the French test tomorrow! I'm not very good at French. I'm sure I ⁰____*won't get*____ the answers right!

Noah Don't worry, you ¹_____ fine! You got a good result in your last test.

Alice Yes, but this is more difficult. I really don't feel well. Maybe I ²_____ to school tomorrow. I ³_____ in bed all day.

Noah That ⁴_____ you. The teacher ⁵_____ you the test on Wednesday.

Alice You're right. But what can I do?

Noah Look, why don't I come round to your place this afternoon after school? We can do some French together. You ⁶_____ that it's not so difficult.

Alice Oh, thanks, Noah.

4 **SPEAKING** Work in pairs. Act out the dialogue in Exercise 3.

⟶ **workbook page 100**

> **PRONUNCIATION**
> The /h/ consonant sound Go to page 121. 🎧

 **VOCABULARY**

Parts of the body

5 Match the words with the photos. Write 1–10 in the boxes.

> 1 ankle | 2 back | 3 elbow | 4 knees | 5 lips | 6 neck | 7 shoulder | 8 stomach | 9 throat | 10 tongue

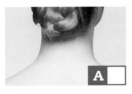 A
 B
 C
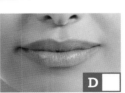 D
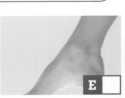 E

 F
 G
 H
 I
 J

6 ◁) 11.04 Listen and match the speakers with the pictures. Write numbers 1–3 in the boxes.   ⟶ **workbook page 102**

 A
 B
 C

🎧 LISTENING

7 Look at the pictures and say what part of the body each person might have a problem with soon.

A

B

C

8 🔊 **11.05** Listen and write the name of the person under each picture.

9 🔊 **11.05** Listen again. Mark the statements T (true) or F (false). Correct the false sentences.

1 Lydia thinks she ate too much. ☐
2 Lydia's dad wants her to do the washing-up. ☐
3 The doctor wants Tim to put some ice on his elbow. ☐
4 The doctor thinks the elbow isn't broken. ☐
5 John can't move his neck at all. ☐
6 The doctor agrees with his grandmother. ☐

10 Put the words in order. Who said each of these sentences? (Dad, Doctor, Lydia, Tim)

1 you / Lydia / all / Are / right
2 all / well / at / not / I'm
3 matter / the / with / What's / you
4 got / really / I've / stomach ache / bad / a
5 really / It's / painful
6 it / hurt / Does

ROLE PLAY At the doctor's

Work in pairs. Student A: Go to page 127. Student B: Go to page 128. Take two or three minutes to prepare. Then have a conversation.

WordWise: Expressions with *do*

11 Complete the sentences from page 103.

1 They'll have to do more _____ together.
2 You should do regular _____ to make sure your muscles are strong.
3 You don't have to do _____ to be healthy and keep fit.

12 Complete each sentence with a word from the list.

cooking | homework | ice cream | well

1 Joe's upstairs – he's doing his _____ .
2 Did you do _____ in your exam?
3 They do great _____ at the new café.
4 Mum has a rest on Sundays and we all do the _____ .

13 **SPEAKING** Complete the questions. Then ask and answer with a partner.

1 _____ you _____ a lot of exercise?
2 Where _____ you _____ your homework?
3 _____ you _____ OK with your homework these days?
4 Who _____ the cleaning in your house?

→ *workbook page 102*

Look 👁️

stomach ache

ear ache

headache

toothache

📖 READING

1 Read the blog quickly. Find a phrase/saying for each of the five pictures.

2 🔊 11.06 Read and listen to the blog. Answer the questions.

1 What is an 'Old Wives' Tale'?
2 Why is it good to eat apples?
3 What did the researchers in New York find out about mothers?
4 What happened to children who ate omega-3 and omega-6?
5 What does the writer think about eating carrots and better night vision?

3 Do you know any more 'Old Wives' Tales'? Tell the class.

ⓖ GRAMMAR
First conditional

4 Match the sentence halves. Check your answers in the blog. Then complete the rule and the table. Choose the correct words.

1 ☐ If you watch a lot of TV,
2 ☐ If you eat cheese at night,
3 ☐ If you eat fish oil,

a you'll have bad dreams.
b you'll get square eyes.
c it will help to prevent heart problems, too.

RULE: Use the first conditional to talk about ⁴**possible** / **certain** events and their ⁵**present** / **future** results.

If clause	Result *clause*
If + present simple,	⁶_____ (*'ll*)
	⁷_____ (*won't*) + base form

It is possible to put the result clause first:
If you fall, you'll hurt yourself. OR
You'll hurt yourself if you fall.

Old Wives' Tales

Old Wives' Tales are those 'helpful' things that your grandparents say that are probably not true. They are things like, 'If you watch a lot of TV, you'll get square eyes', 'If you eat carrots, you'll see well in the dark', or 'If you eat cheese at night, you'll have bad dreams'.

But are they nonsense or is there sometimes a little bit of truth in them? We decided to investigate more.

Let's start with a famous one: 'An apple a day keeps the doctor away'. My grandma said this all the time. Well, of course everyone knows that fruit is an important part of a healthy diet. But can one apple really make a difference? A medical study from 2013 says 'yes'. It found that if people over 50 eat an apple a day, their chances of a heart attack are much smaller than people who don't.

What about 'Gain a child, lose a tooth'? They say that when a woman has a child, a tooth will fall out. Researchers at the New York University College of Dentistry studied more than 2,600 women between the ages of 18 and 64 with one or more children and guess what? They found they had more problems with their teeth than women with no children, although they couldn't say exactly why.

My great uncle was a big believer that 'fish is brain food'. He ate it all the time and he was a clever man, too. It looks like he might be right. Fish have a lot of omega-3 and omega-6 fats in their oil. Some scientists from Oxford studied 120 primary school children, and they discovered that the children who ate omega-3 and omega-6 made big improvements in their schoolwork. If you eat fish oil, it will help to prevent heart problems, too. It seems like eating fish is a good idea.

Finally, what about those carrots? Can they really help your night vision? I've eaten them all my life, but I still walk into things when I get up in the night. Unfortunately, I can't find anything to prove if this is right or wrong. I'll keep looking and I'll let you know as soon as I find out.

5 Put the words in order to make sentences.

0 see Jane / If / tell / I / I'll / her
If I see Jane, I'll tell her.

1 my parents / I'm / will / If / late / be angry

2 I / bring it / I'll / to school tomorrow / If / remember

3 you'll / Jake / come / If / you / meet / to the party

4 rain tomorrow / if / the / it / doesn't / We'll / to / beach / go

5 the concert / if / tonight / I / don't / I / won't / feel better / go / to

6 Complete the first conditional sentences with the correct form of the verbs.

0 If Kate _gives_ (give) me some help, I _I'll finish_ (finish) my homework in an hour.

1 You _____ (not meet) anyone if you _____ (not go out).

2 I _____ (come) to your party if my mum _____ (say) I can.

3 If Ken _____ (not want) his ice cream, I _____ (eat) it.

4 Susan _____ (be) angry if she _____ (hear) about this.

5 If we _____ (buy) hamburgers, we _____ (not have) money for the film.

⟶ **workbook page 101**

Time clauses with *when* / *as soon as*

7 Read the two sentences and answer the questions. Then complete the rule with *will* and *present simple*.

When a woman has a child, a tooth will fall out.
I'll let you know as soon as I find out.

1 What is the difference between *when* and *as soon as*?

2 Do *has* and *find out* refer to the present or the future?

> **RULE:** In sentences about the future, we use the
> 3 _____ form after *if* or *when* or *as soon as*, and
> 4 _____ + base form of the verb in the main clause.

8 Complete the sentences. Use the verbs in the list.

> arrive | finish (x2) | get (x2)

1 As soon as I _____ my exam results, I'll phone you.

2 When I _____ home, I'll check my messages.

3 The party will start as soon as my friend _____ with the music!

4 When the game _____ , we'll go and have a pizza.

5 I'll lend you the book as soon as I _____ reading it.

⟶ **workbook page 101**

VOCABULARY
when and *if*

9 Match sentences 1 and 2 with the explanations.

1 **When I see Martin**, I'll give him your message.

2 **If I see Martin**, I'll give him your message.

a It is possible that I will meet Martin.

b I know that I will meet Martin.

10 Complete the sentences with *if* or *when*.

0 I can't talk to you now. I'll phone you _when_ I get home.

1 A What are you doing tomorrow?
  B _____ there's a good film on, I'll probably go to the cinema.

2 I'm not sure if I want to go to the party tonight. But _____ I decide to go, I'll phone you.

3 It's too hot to go for a walk now. Let's go out in the evening _____ it's cooler.

4 You can watch some TV _____ you finish your homework, and not before!

5 It's the football final tonight. I'll be very happy _____ my team wins.

⟶ **workbook page 102**

LISTENING AND WRITING
A phone message

11 Which of these things do you NOT need to write down if you take a phone message? Mark them with a cross (✗).

1 the name of the caller ☐

2 the telephone number of the person who takes the message ☐

3 the name of the person who the message is for ☐

4 the telephone number of the caller ☐

5 what the caller wants ☐

12 🔊 **11.07** **Listen to a telephone conversation. Complete the message.**

Message from: ¹_____

For: ²_____

Message: she needs ³_____ .

Please ⁴_____

Number to call: ⁵_____

1 🔊 **11.08** Look at the photo. What happened? Where is she now? Listen and read to check.

Luke: Jessica, hi. Oh no! What happened to you?

Jessica: Hi, Luke. Oh, it's so silly. Yesterday, I slipped and fell on the stairs at home. It was my own fault, of course. I mean, I was looking at my phone and not looking where I was going. And now look. A broken leg.

Luke: Poor you! You're lucky it wasn't worse than that.

Jessica: I know, you're right. But I'm so disappointed. And angry, too. It's our cup final match on Saturday, and now I can't play.

Luke: That's a shame. But hey, don't be so hard on yourself. Everyone makes mistakes now and again.

Jessica: I suppose so. But I'm really upset about it anyway.

Luke: Listen. I've got an idea. Can you wait here for a minute or two?

Jessica: Sure. Whatever. But what are you going to do?

Luke: Wait and see!

two minutes later ...

Luke: Right, done, all fixed. How about watching the FA Cup semi-final on Sunday? You know, the match in London. Wembley.

Jessica: What, on TV somewhere?

Luke: No, the real thing. My dad won three tickets to go and see it. He says he can give me two. So how about it? Want to go with us?

Jessica: Seriously? Luke, that's brilliant! I can't wait! Thank you so much!

Luke: No problem. Tell you what, though.

Jessica: What?

Luke: When we go into the stadium, don't start looking at your phone, OK? I don't want you to fall again and break your other leg!

2 🔊 **11.08** Read and listen again. Correct the wrong information.

1 Jessica slipped when she was looking at a book.
2 Now she can't play in the final game on Sunday.
3 They are going to watch the game on TV.
4 Luke is getting three tickets from his father.

Phrases for fluency

3 Find the expressions 1–6 in the dialogue. Who says them? Match them to the definitions a–f.

1 I mean, ...
2 I suppose so.
3 Whatever.
4 Wait and see.
5 I can't wait!
6 Tell you what ...

a What I want to say is ...
b I really don't care.
c Here's what I think ...
d I think that's possibly true.
e You'll know in the future.
f I'm excited about a future event.

4 Complete the mini-dialogues with expressions in Exercise 3.

1 **A** I'm going to see a film on Saturday! _____ !
   B _____ – we could go together. _____ , if that's OK with you.
2 **A** What are you going to give me for my birthday?
   B It's a surprise! _____ .
3 **A** Do you want to go out or stay at home?
   B _____ , Alex.
4 **A** Can I go out tonight, Dad?
   B _____ . But don't be late back, OK?

⚙ FUNCTIONS
Sympathising

KEY LANGUAGE

I'm sorry to hear that.
Poor thing (him / her / John / Sally, etc).
That's a shame.
Poor you.

5 Complete the mini-dialogues using phrases from the Key Language box.

1 **Jessica** Now look! A broken arm!
   Luke _____ .
2 **Jessica** It's our big match on Saturday, and now I can't play.
   Luke _____ .
3 **Luke** Jim, have you heard about Jessica? She broke her arm!
   Jim Really? _____ .
4 **Molly** My granny's very ill.
   Steve _____ her.

6 Read the situations. What can you say in each one?

1 You meet a friend. You know that your friend lost something important yesterday.

Poor you!

2 You hear that someone stole Tim's bike last weekend. You meet Tim's brother.
3 A neighbour says: 'I feel terrible today. I'm ill.'
4 Your friends say they can't come to your party.

LIFE COMPETENCIES

We all have negative feelings sometimes, and it's easy to do or say bad things when we feel like this. Learning what to do when we have negative feelings helps us not make situations worse, or hurt other people and their feelings.

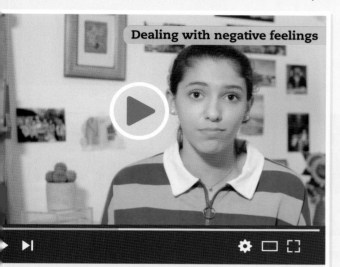

Dealing with negative feelings

1 ▶ 33 **Watch the video. How does she make herself feel better?**

2 ▶ 33 **Watch again and answer the questions.**

1 Which family members make her feel negative?

2 What does Ben do?

3 What are three other things that made her feel unhappy this week?

4 What are two solutions she mentions for dealing with negative feelings?

5 What does she enjoy doing?

3 **Anger is an example of a negative feeling. Read James's story. Why were his parents angry with him?**

My brother, Alex, and I are good friends most of the time. He's only a year older than me, so we like a lot of the same things and share a lot of friends. Sometimes, though, like most brothers, we fight and it can get quite bad.

4 **SPEAKING Work in pairs. Discuss these questions.**

1 What did Alex do to James?

2 How did James feel?

3 What did James do?

4 How did James feel after this?

5 **James threw the book because he was angry with his brother. Which of these actions do you think James should do when he feels angry with his brother in the future?**

> drink water | throw something bigger
> go to his bedroom and sit quietly | shout
> speak to his mum or dad | count to 100
> go for a walk/run | cry

6 **Can you think of more good actions to do when you're angry?**

Me and my world

7 **SPEAKING Think of three things for each list. Then compare with a partner.**

a things that make me feel negative

b things I do when I'm feeling negative

c things I should do when I'm feeling negative

TIPS FOR DEALING WITH NEGATIVE FEELINGS

- Don't react to a bad situation when you are angry about it. Take a break and think calmly about how to react.

- Talk to others. It can help to get a different perspective from a friend.

- If you react badly, learn from it. Think about how you can react differently next time.

Fights often start when we're playing computer games. We both like winning, especially when our friends are with us.

Two months ago, we had a really big fight. I was nervous because I had a violin exam the next week, and so I was practising for an hour or two every day. When I practise, I have to wear my glasses. I wear them for any type of reading or computer work, so it's not strange for Alex to see me wearing them.

Anyway, one day, Alex started calling me 'four–eyes'. At first, I just didn't listen, but after two days, it started to annoy me and I told him to stop. He started laughing and dancing and singing 'Four–eyes! Four–eyes!' I was so angry and wanted him to stop, so I picked up a book that was on the table and threw it at him.

As soon as the book hit Alex in the face, I knew it was bad. Alex and Mum spent six hours at the hospital. Alex's nose was broken. I felt terrible. He didn't speak to me for a week, but Mum and Dad had a lot to say to me.

12 TRAVEL THE WORLD

Get TH!NKING

Watch the video and think: is travelling
just for tourists?
▶34

A

B

C

D

E

F

📖 READING

1 **Match the words with the photos. Write 1–6
   in the boxes.**

> **1** bicycle | **2** boat | **3** bus
> **4** car | **5** plane | **6** train

2 **SPEAKING** **Work in pairs. Ask and answer
  the questions.**

How do you travel …
- to school?
- to the shops?
- to the cinema?
- when you go on holiday?

> *I usually go by bike.*

> *I often take the bus.*

3 **SPEAKING** **Work in pairs or small groups. Which
  type of transport is:**

- cheap?
- expensive?
- exciting?
- dangerous?
- boring?
- your favourite?

4 **Look at the photos and the title of the article on
  page 111. What do you think the article is about?
  Choose one of the following:**

- someone who travels a lot for work
- someone who runs very quickly
- someone who travels more than anyone else

5 🔊 **12.01** **Read and listen to the article to check.**

6 **Read the article again. Correct the information in
  these sentences.**

1 Cassie used one passport to travel round the world.
2 She didn't break the old record by very much.
3 She left her job because she had enough money.
4 Sometimes she didn't go running because she was
   too tired.
5 She talked to tourists about how tourism can
   help countries.
6 She tried to find her American ancestors in
   different countries.
7 She's tired now and doesn't want to travel anymore.
8 She wants to travel to Antarctica for the first time.

A WORLD RECORD BREAKER

by Tom Jenkins

She's taken over 255 flights. She's filled five passports, she's planted trees, has spoken to students in over 40 different countries, and she's funded all $110,000 through sponsors and investors. Now, her amazing adventure has finished and 29-year-old Cassie De Pecol has done it: she's broken two Guinness World records. After 18 months and 10 days, Cassie has become the fastest person to visit every country in the world, and the first woman on record to do so, in half the old record time.

Back in 2014, Cassie decided to leave her job because she wasn't doing what she really wanted to do. What she really wanted to do was to see the world, and she started making plans for her great journey. She started saving all the money she could, and in July 2015, she left home to start her travels. Just over a year and a half later, on 2 February 2017, she arrived in Yemen, the 196th and last country on her (very!) long list.

Of course, she didn't have much time to see each country, but she made sure to use her time well. She spent an average of two to five days in each country. The best parts of her journey included: meeting local people, travelling to remote places on her own, planting trees and educating students on important world issues. Cassie is a keen runner and triathlete and so she also didn't enjoy staying in places where she didn't feel safe enough to go for a run.

But Cassie's journey was not just one long holiday. She also wanted to make a difference. She went as a Peace Ambassador (a special representative) for the International Institute for Peace Through Tourism. In many of the countries she went to, she met and talked to local students – they discussed how tourism can be used to help each country. Cassie is also very worried about the environment, so she agreed to help another organisation called Adventurers and Scientists for Conservation, funded by National Geographic. In many of the countries she went to, she collected samples of water for them to test for the presence of microplastics.

Cassie has always wanted to travel. When she was at school, she had a strong interest in other cultures. She was curious about how Americans have their origins in countries all over the world, and she wanted to find out more about where their ancestors came from. This journey was a chance to start answering some of these questions. So, has she finished her travels now? No, she hasn't – not at all! Cassie hasn't become tired of travelling, and she is already making plans for her next journey. And she didn't forget Antarctica! She visited it on the last stop of her expedition.

TH!NK values

Travel broadens the mind

7 **Read what people said about Cassie De Pecol. Match the comments (1–4) with the values (a–d).**

1 ☐ She's been to every country, so I think she probably understands all kinds of people.

2 ☐ She's probably a better person now because she's learned so many things.

3 ☐ I think it's wonderful that she was an ambassador for Peace Through Tourism.

4 ☐ She wanted to find ancestors, so she's interested in her past and other people's.

a helping to make the world a better place
b self-improvement
c learning about history around the world
d learning about other cultures

8 **SPEAKING** **How important are the values in Exercise 9 for you? Put them in order from 1–4. Compare your ideas in class. Say why you think the values are important or not.**

GRAMMAR
Present perfect simple

1 **Complete the sentences from the article on page 111. Then complete the rule.**

1 She _____ to students in over 40 different countries.
2 She _____ two Guinness World records.
3 Cassie _____ always _____ to travel.
4 _____ she _____ her travels now? No, she _____ .
5 Cassie _____ tired of travelling.

> **RULE:** Use the present perfect to talk about actions that happened sometime in your life up to now. Form the present perfect with the present simple form of ⁶_____ + past participle.

2 **Find other examples of the present perfect in the article on page 111.**

3 **Complete the table.**

Positive	Negative	Questions	Short answers
I/you/we/they 've (¹_____) worked.	I/you/we/they haven't (have not) worked.	⁴_____ I/you/we/ they worked?	Yes, I/you/we/they ⁶_____ . No, I/you/we/they haven't.
He/she/it 's (²_____) worked.	He/she/it hasn't (³_____) worked.	⁵_____ he/she/it worked?	Yes, he/she/it has. No, he/she/it ⁷_____ .

4 **Complete the past participles. Use the irregular verbs list on page 128 of the Workbook to help you.**

base form	past participle
0 be	*been*
1 do	_____
2 go	_____
3 see	_____
4 write	_____
5 meet	_____

base form	past participle
6 speak	_____
7 eat	_____
8 take	_____
9 fly	_____
10 swim	_____
11 win	_____

Look 👁

1 She **has gone** to New York. = She is not here now – she is in New York.
2 She **has been** to New York. = She went to New York and came back (at some time in the past).

5 **Jack and Diane are 25 years old. When they were teenagers, they wanted to do many things – and they have done some of them but not all of them. Look at the table. Complete the sentences about them.**

	learn French	visit Paris	write a book	work in the US	make a lot of money
Diane	✓	✗	✓	✓	✗
Jack	✓	✓	✗	✗	✗

0 Jack and Diane _____*have learned*_____ French.
1 Diane _____ Paris.
2 Diane _____ a book.
3 Jack _____ Paris.
4 Jack _____ in the US.
5 They _____ a lot of money.

6 **WRITING** **Look at the information about Sue and Harry. Write sentences about them.**

	visit another country	fly in a plane	swim in the sea	touch a snake	take a driving test
Sue	✓	✗	✗	✗	✓
Harry	✓	✓	✗	✓	✗

7 **SPEAKING** **Work in pairs. Say things about yourself and people you know. Remember: don't say when in the past.**

> My mother has lived in Africa.
> I've won two tennis competitions.

→ workbook page 108

🎧 LISTENING

8 🔊 **12.02** **Richard Ward is on a radio programme. Listen and choose the correct answers.**

1 Richard is talking about *travelling well / the dangers of travelling.*

2 Richard thinks it's important to *go to famous places / go to places other people don't go.*

3 Richard always takes a scarf with him because *he goes to cold places / he can use it in many different ways.*

9 🔊 **12.02** **Listen again and answer the questions.**

1 When he came home from travelling, where did he stay?

2 How many books has he written?

3 What, for Richard, is the difference between a tourist and a traveller?

4 Why is it good to get lost?

5 What are three things you can do with a scarf?

Ⓖ GRAMMAR

Present perfect with *ever / never*

10 **Complete the sentences with *ever* or *never* and complete the rule.**

1 Have you _____ got lost?

2 I've _____ had my own home.

> **RULE:** When we use the present perfect to talk about experiences and we want to say:
> • 'at no time in (my) life' we use the word ³_____
> • 'at any time in (your) life' we use the word ⁴_____
> The words ***ever*** and ***never*** usually come between *have* and the past participle.

11 **Complete the mini-dialogues with the words in the list.**

> been | eaten | ever | have
> never | no | played | yes

1 **A** Have you _____ watched a silent film?
  B Yes, I _____ .

2 **A** Have you ever _____ to the Olympic Games?
  B _____ , I've never been to them.

3 **A** Have you ever _____ tennis?
  B _____ , I have.

4 **A** Have you ever _____ a really hot curry?
  B No, I've _____ tried curry.

→ *workbook page 109*

⚙ FUNCTIONS

Talking about life experiences

12 **Work in pairs. Ask and answer the questions.**

1 ever / see / a snake?

2 ever / eat / something horrible?

3 ever / be / on television?

4 ever / speak / to someone from the US?

5 ever / win / a prize?

6 ever / be / to another country?

> *Have you ever seen a snake?*

> *Yes, I have. It was a python at the zoo.*

> *No, I haven't.*

💬 SPEAKING

13 **Work in pairs. Think of a famous person. Ask about things that the famous person has done in their life and imagine the answers. Use some of the verbs in the list.**

> drive | eat | play | see
> stay | travel | win | write

> *Mr President – have you ever eaten fried spiders?*

> *Yes, I have. I eat them all the time.*

Train to TH!NK

Exploring differences

14 **SPEAKING** **Work in small groups. Look at the pairs of things. Answer the questions.**

a What is the same?

b What is different?

1 A car and a taxi

2 A train and a plane

3 A holiday and a journey

4 A tourist and a traveller

The same: a car and a taxi have wheels / doors / a driver.

Different: you drive your car, but a taxi driver drives the taxi. In a taxi, you have to pay.

15 **SPEAKING** **Compare your ideas with others in the class.**

> **PRONUNCIATION**
> Sentence stress Go to page 121.

TRAVELLING THE WORLD
FROM YOUR SOFA!

Seventeen-year-old Tom Davidson hasn't left his home since he was 15. The last time he went out was two years ago. He was walking to catch a bus when he was hit on the head by a sign falling from a building. He spent more than two months in hospital and doctors told him he was lucky to be alive. The accident left Tom with agoraphobia: the idea of being outdoors makes him feel extremely anxious.

The problem is that Tom loves travelling. Before his accident, Tom spent most weekends exploring his home city of London by bus, underground train and his scooter, and he looked forward to holidays abroad with his parents. Now the idea of driving in a car to France or taking a plane to Italy terrifies him.

However, there is a way that Tom can still visit the most remote corners of the world without leaving the security of his home: Google Maps. In the last year and a half, Tom has visited every country in the world where Google Maps has been and taken photos. Using 'street view', he has walked down the streets of the world's most famous cities, he has seen all the world's most amazing geographical features and he has visited places in the world that he didn't know existed: all of this from the comfort of his home.

Tom's virtual travel is more than just a hobby – it has become an art project. He has taken more than 5,000 screenshots of places he has visited and last week, there was an exhibition of his best photos at a school near his home (but of course, he didn't go). Tom also hopes that his online journeys will help him eventually to overcome his agoraphobia. As he discovers more places that he wants to visit one day, he is becoming more and more determined to leave his home. And his dream, if he can, is to work in the travel industry, for example as a flight attendant or a tour guide.

 READING

1 **Read the text quickly. Find out:**
- what problem Tom has got
- what he uses to 'travel'
- what his dream for the future is

2 **◁) 12.05 Read and listen to the text. Correct the wrong information.**
1 Tom hasn't left his home for three years.
2 His agoraphobia started when he was hit by a car.
3 Before the accident, he often went on holiday with his parents in London.
4 Using Google Maps, he has visited every country in the world.
5 Tom uses 'street view' to go to places that he knows about.
6 Tom hopes that in the future he can get a job with Google Maps.

3 SPEAKING **Work in two groups. Group A: you are tour guides. Group B: you are flight attendants. In your group, think of answers to these questions.**
1 When did you start your job?
2 Tell us about a problem you've had.
3 Tell us about a funny moment you've had.
4 Do you like your job or do you want to change?

4 SPEAKING **Work in pairs – one student from Group A with one student from Group B. Ask and answer the questions.**

5 SPEAKING **Decide whose answers were best: the tour guide's or the flight attendant's.**

GRAMMAR
Present perfect vs. past simple

6 Complete the sentences from the article on page 114. Complete the rule with the names of the tenses.

1 The last time he _____ out was two years ago.
2 He _____ down the streets of the world's most famous cities.
3 Before his accident, Tom _____ most weekends exploring his home city of London.
4 He _____ more than 5,000 screenshots.
5 Tom's virtual travel is more than just a hobby – it _____ an art project.
6 Last week, there _____ an exhibition of his best photos at a school near his home.

> **RULE:** Use the [7]_____ to talk about situations or actions at a particular time in the past. Use the [8]_____ to talk about situations or actions in the past, when we don't say when they happened.

VOCABULARY
Transport and travel

0 *a minibus*

3 _____

1 _____

4 _____

2 _____

5 _____

7 Find more examples of verbs in the past simple and present perfect in the article on page 114.

8 Choose the correct forms.

My name's Michael Edwards and I'm 26.
[1]*I've been / I was* very lucky in my life because I have a good job and I travel a lot for work.
[2]*I've lived / I lived* in three different countries: Thailand, India and Singapore.
[3]*I've lived / I lived* in Singapore from 2017 to 2019. I live in Thailand now.
[4]*I've got / I got* married two years ago. My wife and I travel a lot together and [5]*we've seen / we saw* some wonderful places. Last year, [6]*we've seen / we saw* the Taj Mahal in India.
[7]*I've done / I did* some crazy things in my life, but the craziest was last month –
[8]*I've gone / I went* by minibus all the way to the north of Thailand. [9]*It's been / It was* really exciting!

→ workbook page 109

9 🔊 **12.06** Write the words under the photos. Listen and check.

> a minibus | a helicopter | a tram | a motorbike
> a scooter | an underground train

Travel verbs

10 Complete the sentences with the correct form of the verbs in the list.

> catch | drive | fly | miss | ride | take

0 I had to walk home because I *missed* the bus.
1 I ran very fast, but I didn't _____ the train.
2 I have never _____ in a helicopter.
3 My brother's got a motorbike and now he's learning to _____ it.
4 We got in the car and we _____ to France.
5 The rain was terrible, so we _____ a taxi.

11 **SPEAKING** Work in pairs. Ask each other questions. Use the verbs in Exercise 10 and the forms of transport you can see on this page and page 110.

Have you ever flown in a helicopter?

No, I haven't. Have you ever taken a tram?

Yes, I took a tram in Lisbon when I was on holiday.

→ workbook page 110

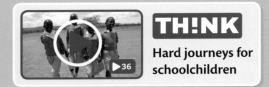

TH!NK
Hard journeys for schoolchildren
▶36

A

B

Culture

1 **Look at the photos and answer the questions. Then say what you think the article is going to be about.**

Where can you see ...
- a student riding to school on a donkey?
- children walking to school along some rail tracks?

2 🔊 **12.07** **Read and listen to the article and say which country each photo is from.**

HARD JOURNEYS
FOR SCHOOLCHILDREN

'How do you get to school?' This question often gets an answer like 'By bus' or 'I walk' or 'My parents take me by car'. But not always – there are children in many different parts of the world who, every day, have to go on a difficult journey in order to get to their lessons. They travel for kilometres on foot, or by boat, bicycle, donkey or train. They cross deserts, mountains, rivers, snow and ice: for example, the children of the Iñupiat community in Alaska go to school and then come back when it is dark, in extremely cold temperatures. And they are not the only ones. Kids in many countries do this and more.

These children in Indonesia have to cross a bridge ten metres above a dangerous river to get to their class on time. (Some years ago the bridge fell down after very heavy rain.) Then they walk many more kilometres through the forest to their school in Banten.

A pupil at Gulu Village Primary School, China, rides a donkey as his grandfather walks beside him. Gulu is a mountain village in a national park. The school is far away from the village. It is halfway up a mountain, so it takes five hours to climb from the bottom of the mountain to the school. The children have a dangerous journey: the path is only 45 centimetres wide in some places.

In Sri Lanka, some children have to cross a piece of wood between two walls of an old castle every morning. Their teacher watches them carefully. But in Galle, Sri Lanka, many girls don't go to school – they have to go to work or get married young. So girls are happy to take a risk in order to get to school.

Six-year-old Fabricio Oliveira gets on his donkey every morning to ride with his friends for over an hour through a desert region in the very dry Sertão area of northeast Brazil. Their school is in Extrema. It's a tiny village – very few people live there.

These children live in houses on Chetla Road in Delhi, India. Their homes are near the busy and dangerous railway lines that go to Alipur station. Every morning they walk along the tracks to get to their school, 40 minutes away.

So one question we can ask is: why do the children do this? Because their parents make them do it? The answer, in many cases, is no – it's because for them going to school means a better future: they hope to get a job and money so they can help their families and their neighbours. And this is why rivers, deserts or danger won't stop them on their way to school.

C

3 **Read the article again. What difficulties do children in these places face to get to school?**

1 the children of the Iñupiat community in Alaska
2 the children who go to the school in Banten, Indonesia
3 the children who go to Gulu Village Primary School, China
4 the children who go to school in Galle, Sri Lanka
5 fabricio Oliveira in Brazil
6 the children who live along Chetla Road in Delhi, India

4 **VOCABULARY** **There are eight highlighted words in the article. Match the words with these meanings. Write the words.**

0 from one side to the other   *wide*
1 people living in houses near you   _____
2 a trip   _____
3 do something that can be dangerous   _____
4 a group of houses usually in the countryside   _____
5 the things that trains move on   _____
6 very, very small   _____
7 not late   _____

5  **SPEAKING** **Which journey do you think is the most difficult? Compare with others in the class.**

✏️ WRITING
Someone I admire

1 **INPUT** **Read Javed's essay about 'Someone I admire'. Answer the questions.**

1 When and where was his aunt Priti born?
2 Where does she live now and when did she move there?
3 How does she travel in her work?
4 What does she want to do in the future?
5 Why does Javed admire his aunt?

2 **Find examples in the essay of the word *in* with these things.**

1 a year   3 a city
2 a month   4 a country

3 **ANALYSE** **Look at the four paragraphs of Javed's essay about his aunt. Match the paragraphs with the contents.**

Paragraph 1   a what she does and how
Paragraph 2   b why he admires her
Paragraph 3   c when and where she was born
Paragraph 4   d why she does these things

Someone I admire

(1) My Aunt Priti is a really great woman. She was born in England in 1980, in a city called Leicester, but now she lives and works in Angola. She went to Angola in 2014.

(2) My aunt is a doctor and she worked at a hospital in Birmingham for a few years. But in 2014, she decided to go and work in small villages in Angola because she heard that they needed doctors. She travels from village to village to help people. She has a small car that she uses. Sometimes, though, she goes in a very small plane because the roads aren't good enough.

(3) Aunt Priti says that she wants to stay there because there is a lot of work to do. She has also met a man there — she told me in an email that they are getting married in July next year. Aunt Priti hopes that she can help to teach Angolan people to become doctors in the future. She has learned a lot of Portuguese there, too — that can't be easy!

(4) I said before that she's a great woman. Why do I think that? Well, because she is helping other people and is happy doing that, and because she has learned a lot about another culture.

4 **PLAN** **Think of someone that you admire: a famous person; or someone you know in your own life; or someone you invent.**

For the person, think about:
• facts about their life (when they were born, etc.)
• what they do, where and how, when they started
• what they want to do in the future
• why you admire them

5 **PRODUCE** **Write an essay called 'Someone I admire' in about 150 words. Use the example essay and language above to help you.**

A2 Key for Schools

→ workbook page 115

READING AND WRITING
Part 3: 3-option multiple choice

1 **For each question, choose the correct answer.**

Hotels in
Sydney, Australia

The Green Hotel (7/10)

Place
The Green Hotel is downtown and is walking distance to many restaurants, cafés and shops. It's a long way from the airport. It's also on a busy road, but you don't hear traffic noise in the rooms (but noise from other guests can be a problem at night). There aren't any really good views from the hotel, but the garden at the back is nice.

Style & character
The hotel is popular, mostly with young people, so you can meet other travellers. The staff are pleasant, helpful and of course speak English and one or two other languages, too. It's a clean place and there's a sitting room for guests to sit and talk in.

Rooms
Some rooms have a bathroom, and of course they're the best. All the rooms are quite small, but have a table and a reading lamp. See above about noise. The beds are small but comfortable and everything is very clean.

Food
The only meal you can have at the hotel is breakfast. It's included in the price and not at all bad. There is a good choice of fruit, cheese, cereals and bread. Eggs are freshly cooked for a small extra charge.

Value for money
For people who can't pay high prices, this is a good choice. Room prices are quite cheap. At popular times of the year (October to January) there is a minimum three-night stay. Check the website for more details.

1 Where is The Green Hotel?
  A It isn't far from the airport.
  B It is near the city centre.
  C It is opposite a large garden.

2 Guests at the hotel
  A speak many different languages.
  B can sit in the sitting room to talk.
  C are usually old people.

3 In the rooms,
  A you can hear other guests.
  B there's always a bathroom.
  C the beds are all large.

4 What does the article say about breakfast?
  A It's expensive.
  B It's pretty good.
  C It's very bad.

5 What does the article say about prices?
  A The hotel is more expensive in the high season.
  B Guests pay more if they only stay for two nights.
  C The rooms don't cost very much all year long.

Part 5: Open cloze

→ workbook page 97

2 **For each question, write the correct answer.**
Write one word for each gap.

Hey!
For today's blog, I'm going ^{0} _to_ talk about my next trip. I love travelling and seeing different cultures. So far, I've ^{1}_____ to 56 countries. Next year, if I have enough money, I'm going to buy ^{2}_____ aeroplane ticket and visit Thailand.
I'm excited about this journey. I've ^{3}_____ been to Asia before. First, I'm going to ^{4}_____ to Bangkok from my home, Sydney. When I arrive, I'm going to take a taxi to my aunt's house. ^{5}_____ my plan goes well, I will travel through Thailand on the Chao Phraya River by ^{6}_____ .

LISTENING
Part 5: Matching

→ workbook page 61

3 **◁)) 12.08 For each question, choose the correct answer.**

You will hear Jack talking to a friend about his transport project. How does each person get to school?

Example
0 Jack   [E]   **E** on foot

People		**Transport**
		A bike
1 Olivia	☐	**B** boat
2 Rashid	☐	**C** bus
3 Morris	☐	**D** car
4 Leslie	☐	**E** on foot
5 Adam	☐	**F** scooter
		G taxi
		H train

 VOCABULARY

1 Complete the sentences with the words in the list. There are two extra words.

back | caught | flew | helicopter | lip | missed | neck | ride | scooter | stomach ache | tongue | trams

1 He's really rich. He goes to work by _____ and he lands on the roof of his office building.
2 I've got a _____ . I think I ate something bad for lunch.
3 We _____ the last train home, so we walked home.
4 Open your mouth. I want to take a look at your _____ .
5 I can't _____ a motorbike, but I really want to learn how to. I think they're great.
6 I fell and cut my mouth and made my top _____ bleed.
7 My dad rides his _____ to work. It's quicker than going by car and a lot cheaper.
8 We _____ over the sea and the beaches in a small plane. The views were fantastic!
9 I never sleep on my _____ .
10 Many cities are now using _____ to get people to and from work.

/10

GRAMMAR

2 Put the words in order to make sentences.

1 phone / I'll / home / you / get / soon / as / I / as
2 taxi / I / train / miss / if / the / take / a / I'll
3 ever / Have / Argentina / you / been / to
4 seen / She's / sea / never / the
5 different / six / lived / cities / in / They've
6 grandchildren / be / easy / for / won't / our / Life

3 Find and correct the mistake in each sentence.

1 She's played volleyball yesterday.
2 If we will be late, the teacher will be angry.
3 I have ever broken an arm or a leg.
4 I've never gone to Japan.
5 She has took a lot of photos on holiday.
6 One day in the future people will living on the moon.

/12

FUNCTIONAL LANGUAGE

4 Write the missing words.

1 A What's the _____ ?
  B My back _____ a lot.
2 A I've _____ a headache.
  B I'm sorry to _____ that. Would you like some medicine?
3 A Have you _____ been to France?
  B No, I _____ .
4 A Do you think it _____ rain this afternoon?
  B I don't know. I'm not _____ .

/8

MY SCORE /30

22–30  10–21 0–9

119

PRONUNCIATION

UNIT 7
Vowel sounds: /ʊ/ and /uː/

1 **◁)) 7.07** **Listen to the dialogue.**

Luke Let's look in this room, Sue.

Sue Wow! It's got things from the moon in it.

Luke Look at these cool boots! I saw them in our science book.

Sue We should take a photo for our school project, Luke.

2 **Say the words with the short /ʊ/ vowel sound. Then say the words with the long /uː/ vowel sound.**

3 **◁)) 7.08** **Listen and repeat. Then practise with a partner.**

UNIT 8
Strong and weak forms of *was* and *were*

1 **◁)) 8.02** **Listen to the dialogue.**

Girl Was she shopping?

Boy Yes, she was. She was shopping for socks.

Girl Were they doing their homework?

Boy No, they weren't. They were learning to surf!

2 **Say the words with the /ɒ/ sound. Now say the words with the /ɜː/ sound. When *was* and *were* aren't stressed, we use the /ə/ sound. It's the same as /ɜː/ but shorter.**

3 **◁)) 8.03** **Listen and repeat. Then practise with a partner.**

UNIT 9
Vowel sounds: /ɪ/ and /aɪ/

1 **◁)) 9.05** **Listen to the dialogue.**

Jill I'd like to live in the wild. What about you, Mike?

Mike I prefer a city lifestyle. I don't like lions or tigers – or insects!

Jill But living in the wild's much more exciting!

Mike Yes, Jill – and it's more frightening, too.

2 **Say the words with the short /ɪ/ vowel sound. Then say the words with the long /aɪ/ vowel sound.**

3 **◁)) 9.06** **Listen and repeat. Then practise with a partner.**

UNIT 10
Voiced /ð/ and unvoiced /θ/ consonants

1 **◁)) 10.04** **Listen to the dialogue.**

Beth Look – there's the theatre.

Harry That's not the right one, Beth.

Beth Well, it says, 'The Fifth Avenue Theatre.'

Harry But we want the one on Third Street!

2 **Say the words with the voiced /ð/. Then say the words with the unvoiced /θ/.**

3 **◁)) 10.05** **Listen and repeat. Then practise with a partner.**

UNIT 11
The /h/ consonant sound

1 **◁)) 11.02** **Listen to the dialogue.**

Dr Harris Who's next? Oh, hello Harry. How can I help you?

Harry Well, Dr Harris – my head's very hot!

Dr Harris Let me see … does it hurt here?

Harry Yes, doctor! That feels horrible!

Dr Harris It's your hat, Harry. It's too small!

2 **Say the words starting with the /h/ consonant sound.**

3 **◁)) 11.03** **Listen and repeat. Then practise with a partner.**

UNIT 12
Sentence stress

1 **◁)) 12.03** **Listen to the stress in these sentences.**

<u>Car</u> – <u>plane</u> – <u>bike</u> – <u>train</u>.
A <u>car</u>, a <u>plane</u>, a <u>bike</u>, a <u>train</u>.
A <u>car</u> and a <u>plane</u> and a <u>bike</u> and a <u>train</u>.
A <u>car</u> and then a <u>plane</u> and then a <u>bike</u> and then a <u>train</u>.

2 **Which words are stressed in every sentence? What happens to the other words?**

3 **◁)) 12.04** **Listen and repeat. Then practise with a partner.**

UNIT 7
have to / don't have to

> We always use the base form of the verb after **have to / don't have to**.
> ✓ He **has to tidy** his room today.
> ✗ He has to ~~tidied~~ his room today.
> ✗ He has to ~~tidying~~ his room today.
>
> We use the correct form of **do + not/n't + have to** to say that something isn't necessary. We don't use **haven't to**.
> ✓ You **don't have to help** me. I can do it.
> ✗ You ~~haven't to~~ help me. I can do it.

Find six mistakes. Correct them.

I have to do a lot of housework at home, but I'm OK about that. I have to tidying my room, but I haven't to vacuum the floor. My brother has to does that. We have to do the washing up, but we don't have do the washing. My dad does that once a week. I haven't to do the cooking – my mum likes cooking. She says it helps her to relax. Of course, I have to doing my homework every day after school. I'm not OK about that!

UNIT 8
Past continuous vs. past simple

> We use the past continuous to talk about background actions in the past, and the past simple for actions which happened at one moment in the past.
> ✓ I **was watching** television when the lights **went** out.
> ✗ I ~~watched~~ television when the lights went out.

Complete the story with the past continuous or past simple of the verb in brackets.

The surprise!

It ¹_____ (happen) last Saturday while I ²_____ (have) a party at my house. At 9 o'clock, we ³_____ (dance) and having a fantastic time. Then, suddenly, the lights ⁴_____ (go) out. I ⁵_____ (close) my eyes and screamed! But when I ⁶_____ (stop), I heard that all my friends ⁷_____ (laugh). When I ⁸_____ (open) my eyes, everybody was smiling at me. When my mum ⁹_____ (arrive) with a cake and candles, I finally understood …

UNIT 9
Comparative adjectives

> We use **more** + adjective with two syllables or more to form the comparative. We don't use **more** with adjectives with one syllable or with adjectives that are already in the comparative form (e.g. *smaller, colder, friendlier*).
> ✓ His room is **smaller** than mine.
> ✗ His room is ~~more small~~ than mine.
> ✗ His room is ~~more smaller~~ than mine.

Choose the correct sentence.

1. a Lions can run more faster during the night.
   b Lions can run faster during the night.
2. a The weather in the Kalahari is drier than in Europe.
   b The weather in the Kalahari is more dry than in Europe.
3. a It's more hotter in the summer than in the winter.
   b It's hotter in the summer than in the winter.
4. a People in the countryside are friendlier than people in the city.
   b People in the countryside are more friendlier than people in the city.

can / can't for ability

> We always use the base form of the verb after **can / can't**.
> ✓ He **can swim**, but he **can't surf**.
> ✗ He can ~~swam~~, but he can't ~~to surf~~.

Choose the correct verb form.

1. I love living by the sea. On sunny days, I can *went / going / go* to the beach.
2. On cold days, you can *do / doing / to do* the shopping in the town centre.
3. We can *learning / learn / to learn* a lot about wildlife from nature programmes.
4. You can't *drive / driving / drove* a car if you're 15.
5. They can't *to come / coming / come* to the party because they're on holiday.

UNIT 10
be going to for intentions

> We use the present tense of *be* + *going to* + base form of the verb to talk about our intentions in the future. Remember to use the present tense of *be*.
>
> ✓ He **is going to study** all weekend.
>
> ✗ He ~~going~~ to study all weekend.

Complete the sentences with *be going to* and the verb in brackets.

1 He _____ (paint) his bedroom on Saturday.
2 I've bought a new chair. I _____ (put) it near the TV.
3 We _____ (visit) my cousin because he is ill.
4 They _____ (go) to the sports centre by car.
5 We _____ (watch) a film tonight.

Present continuous for arrangements

> We use the present continuous to talk about arrangements for the future. We don't use the present simple.
>
> ✓ I'm **going to visit** my grandparents tomorrow.
>
> ✗ I ~~go~~ to visit my grandparents tomorrow.
>
> To ask questions about arrangements, we use question word + *be* + subject + the *-ing* form of the verb. Remember to put the words in the correct order.
>
> ✓ What **are you doing** tomorrow?
>
> ✗ What ~~you are doing~~ tomorrow?

Find six mistakes in the dialogue. Correct them.

Lara Hi, Sam, what you are doing on Saturday?

Sam Well, in the morning, I play football in the park.

Lara What are you doing in the afternoon?

Sam I don't do anything. What are you doing?

Lara I paint my bedroom.

Sam Cool! What colour do you use?

Lara I'm going to choose the colour when I go to the shop.

Sam Which shop are you going to?

Lara I go to the shop in the high street at 2 o'clock.

Sam OK. I'll meet you there! I can help you to choose.

UNIT 11
will / *won't* for future predictions

> We use the present continuous to talk about things happening now and future arrangements. We use *will* or *won't* + base form to make future predictions.
>
> ✓ I'm sure you**'ll do** well in your test next week.
>
> ✗ I'm sure you ~~are doing~~ well in your test next week.
>
> ✓ I'm **going** to a party on Saturday.
>
> ✗ I ~~will go~~ to a party on Saturday.

Choose present continuous or *'ll* / *won't* to complete the email.

UNIT 12
Present perfect simple

> We use the present perfect simple to talk about situations or actions that happened at some time in the past.
>
> ✓ I **have met** a lot of famous actors.
>
> ✗ I ~~met~~ a lot of famous actors.
>
> We use the past simple to talk about situations or actions at a specific time in the past.
>
> ✓ A year ago, I **met** a famous actor.
>
> ✗ A year ago, I ~~have met~~ a famous actor.

Find seven mistakes in the text. Correct them.

My parents work for international companies, so I travelled a lot. I've lived in Europe, Asia and the US. Two years ago, I have lived in Spain for six months. My brother's only three, so he only went to Europe and he forgot that trip! My dad travelled to more places. He has been to Australia and New Zealand last year, but we never visited England.

STUDENT A

UNIT 7, PAGE 72

Student A

You are a son or daughter. You are at home.

You want to see a friend.

You are phoning your mum or dad about it.

When your mum/dad tells you that you should do some housework, ask her/him what you have to do.

Also, tell your mum/dad that there are some things she/he shouldn't forget. When she/he asks you what things, say:

She/He …

- should do the shopping
- shouldn't be late tonight (you want to watch a film together with her/him)
- mustn't forget to bring some chocolate biscuits!

The line is not very good, so you have to ask your mum or dad several times to repeat what she/he has said.

UNIT 11, PAGE 105

Student A

1 You are a patient and Student B is a doctor. Choose one of the pictures here. Tell Student B about your problem. Have the conversation.

2 Now Student B is the patient and you are the doctor. Ask Student B about their problem. Have the conversation.

STUDENT B

UNIT 7, PAGE 72

Student B

You are a mum or dad. Your son/daughter is phoning you.

Make sure he/she knows that he/she has to do some housework before he/she can go out. When he/she asks you, say:

He/She …

- has to tidy up his/her room
- should load the dishwasher
- mustn't forget to vacuum the floor

When your son or daughter tells you that there are things you shouldn't forget, ask them what things.

The line is not very good, so you have to ask your son or daughter several times to repeat what he/she has said.

UNIT 11, PAGE 105

Student B

1 You are a doctor and Student A is a patient. Ask Student A about their problem. Have the conversation.

2 Now you are the patient and Student A is the doctor. Choose one of the pictures here. Tell the doctor about your problem. Have the conversation.

owledgements

authors and publishers acknowledge the following sources of copyright
rial and are grateful for the permissions granted. While every effort has been
e, it has not always been possible to identify the sources of all the material
or to trace all copyright holders. If any omissions are brought to our notice,
ill be happy to include the appropriate acknowledgements on reprinting and
e next update to the digital edition, as applicable.

U = Unit.

Cassandra De Pecol for the text about her travel. Reproduced with permission.

ography

e photographs are sourced from Getty Images.

Creative Crop/Photodisc; sweetym/E+; larigan-Patricia Hamilton/Moment
; hocus-focus/iStock/Getty Images Plus Unreleased; Wong Sze Fei/EyeEm;
/iStock/Getty Images Plus; ahmetemre/iStock/Getty Images Plus; hadynyah/
ler84/iStock/Getty Images Plus; Grassetto/iStock/Getty Images Plus; Image
ce; Saklakova/iStock/Getty Images Plus; hh5800/E+; Sharon Gallo/iStock/
Images Plus Editorial; sh22/iStock/Getty Images Plus; Dave King/Dorling
ersley/Getty Images Plus; Andregric/iStock/Getty Images Plus; Juanmonino/
yan McVay/DigitalVision; Fuse/Corbis; esemelwe/E+; Glow Images, Inc/
Images Plus; Maskot; Anthony-Masterson/Photolibrary/Getty Images Plus;
rthand/E+; PeopleImages/E+; Ryan Smedstad/EyeEm; Thanasis Zovoilis/
ent Open; **U8:** Caiaimage/Chris Ryan; John P Kelly/Stone; SOPA Images/
Rocket; microgen/iStock/Getty Images Plus; Petr_Joura/iStock/Getty Images
Paul Bradbury/Caiaimage; Getty Images Sport; Central Press/Hulton Archive;
Valton/Getty Images Sport; Alistair Berg/DigitalVision; Daniel Milchev/
mage Bank; nattrass/E+; dmbaker/iStock/Getty Images Plus; Razvan Chisu/
n; simonkr/E+; Petri Oeschger/Moment; ultramarinfoto/E+; Artranq/
/Getty Images Plus; South_agency/E+; Frans Lemmens/Corbis Unreleased;
noto; sampics/Corbis Sport; Ryan_Wai/iStock Editorial/Getty Images Plus;
truction Photography/Avalon/Hulton Archive; **U9:** Christopher Gandy/
ent Open; Vladimir Naumoff/500Px Plus; Milko Marchetti/500px; john finney
ography/Moment; Todd Ryburn Photography/Moment; GomezDavid/E+;
m Manning/Corbis Documentary; Hoberman Collection/Universal Images
p; Eric Vandeville/Gamma-Rapho; NurPhoto; trendobjects/iStock/Getty
es Plus; skodonnell/iStock/Getty Images Plus Unreleased; View Stock; alle12/
10: Nikada/iStock/Getty Images Plus; lpbb/Moment Open; John Moore/Getty
es News; Istvan Kadar Photography/Moment; Yukinori Hasumi/Moment; C
ed Studios/Photodisc; zhangshuang/Moment; juanestey/iStock/Getty Images
Thomas Trutschel/Photothek; onfilm/E+; DreamPictures/The Image Bank;
Cade/The Image Bank; Dan Brownsword/Cultura; Hein von Horsten/Gallo
s; Loop Images/Universal Images Group; **U11:** malyugin/iStock/360/Getty
es; AntonioGuillem/iStock/360/Getty Images; Hlib Shabashnyi/iStock/360/
Images; Viktor_Gladkov/iStock/360/Getty Images; Teeramet Thanomkiat/
n; Eric Audras/Onoky; ljubaphoto/E+; Ismailciydem/E+; Jose Luis Pelaez/
disc; **U12:** Aaron Foster/DigitalVision; Chris Mellor/Lonely Planet Images;
d Andronov/iStock/Getty Images Plus; Marin Tomas/Moment; olaser/E+;
las Sacha/Moment Open; GregorBister/iStock/Getty Images Plus; RogiervdE/
/Getty Images Plus; Halfdark/fStop; Copyright Artem Vorobiev/Moment;
Daniela/Moment; Alexandr Konovalov/iStock/Getty Images Plus Editorial;
gato/iStock/Getty Images Plus Editorial; Westend61; Natal'â Maâk/EyeEm;
rat/E+; Stefanie Grewel/Cultura; AFP; Shammi Mehra/AFP; ER Productions
ed/DigitalVision.

photography by Antonio Ferreira Silva/EyeEm/Getty Images; PeopleImages/
/Getty Images Plus/Getty Images

ollowing images are sourced from other sources.

auremar/Shutterstock; Dudarev Mikhail/Shutterstock; Halfpoint/Shutterstock;
gerix/Shutterstock; Marco Prati/Shutterstock; **U12:** Expedition 196, LLC.
andra de Pecol); Sipa Press/REX.

rations

a Nyari (Beehive Illustration) pp. 78, 100; Amit Tayal (Beehive Illustration)
; Tom Heard (The Bright Agency) pp. 68, 69, 79, 94, 104, 105, 112, 127, 128;
a Lakicevic (Beehive Illustration) p. 98; Arunas Kacinskas and John Goodwin
Candy Illustration) p. 82; Szabolcs Pal (Beehive Illustration) pp. 70, 89; Martin
rs (Beehive Illustration) pp. 86, 102, 111; Adam Linley (Beehive Illustration) p.
aham Kennedy p. 103.

mentary video stills

e stills are sourced from Getty Images.

shih-wei/Creatas Video+/Getty Images Plus; **p. 74:** Caiafilm/Vetta;
Barry Lewis/Corbis Historical; **p. 84:** anneypyang/Creatas Video+/Getty
s Plus; **p. 92:** loveguli/Creatas Video; **p. 98:** DEA/A. DAGLI ORTI/De Agostini
e Library/Getty Images Plus; **p. 102:** SVTeam/Creatas Video+/Getty Images
. **110:** miodrag ignjatovic/Creatas Video; **p. 116:** Hugh Sitton/one80:
ture.

Video Stills

All the video stills are sourced from Getty Images.

U7: Zolotaosen/iStock/Getty Images Plus; NurPhoto; Norberto Duarte/AFP;
Reimphoto/iStock/Getty Images Plus; **U8b:** Peter Unger/Lonely Planet Images;
Christian Heeb/AWL Images; Barry Lewis/Corbis Historical; Warren Little/Getty
Images Sport; AFP; Rene Johnston/Toronto Star; Christophe Archambault/AFP;
U10b: PacoRomero/E+; Archive Photos; DEA/A. Dagli Orti/De Agostini Picture
Library; Christophel Fine Art/Universal Images Group; Michael Nicholson/Corbis
Historical; benoitb/DigitalVision Vectors; steved_np3/iStock/Getty Images Plus;
susandaniels/iStock/Getty Images Plus; **U11:** David Gifford/Science Photo Library/
Science Photo Library; Rosdiana Ciaravolo/Getty Images Entertainment; **U12b:** Gary
Friedman/Los Angeles Times.

Vlog & Grammar Rap video stills: Silversun Media Group.

Full video acknowledgements can be found in the online Teacher's Resources.

Audio Production: Leon Chambers.

This page is intentionally left blank.

WORKBOOK
COMBO B
1
CEFR
A2

TH!NK
SECOND EDITION

Herbert Puchta,
Jeff Stranks &
Peter Lewis-Jones
with Clare Kennedy

CAMBRIDGE
UNIVERSITY PRESS

This page is intentionally left blank.

CONTENTS

7 SMART LIFE

GRAMMAR
have to / don't have to   → SB p.68

1 ★☆☆ **Match the sentences with the signs.**

0 You don't have to go to Terminal A for your flight. `d`

1 You have to wash your hands. ☐

2 Drivers have to turn right here. ☐

3 You have to go straight ahead. ☐

4 You have to leave your dog outside. ☐

5 Children don't have to pay. ☐

2 ★★☆ **Put the words in order to make sentences.**

0 the / a lot / have / We / Maths / study / test / to / for
We have to study a lot for the Maths test.

1 be / to / to / creative / have / find / answer / You / the
_____

2 Sundays / make / to / has / he / On / breakfast
_____

3 early / they / get / have / Do / to / up /
_____

4 Lucas / school / tomorrow / have / doesn't / to / to / go
_____

5 have / I / phone / Do / to / you /
_____

6 me / to / You / have / help / don't
_____

3 ★★☆ **Match the questions with the answers.**

0 Does your dad have to travel a lot in his job? `d`
1 Can I come to your place tomorrow? ☐
2 Why can't Sophie come with us to the beach? ☐
3 Does your sister live in the city centre? ☐
4 Can I go to the match on Sunday? ☐
5 Why can't I go to the cinema tonight? ☐

a I spoke to her mum. She has to help at home.
b No, she doesn't. She has to take a train every day.
c I'm afraid you can't. We have to visit Grandma.
d Yes. He goes to other countries quite a lot.
e Because you have to tidy up your room.
f No, I'm sorry. You have to study for school.

4 ★★★ **Answer the questions so they are true for you.**

1 Do you have to get up early on weekdays?
_____
_____

2 Do you have to switch off your phone at school?
_____
_____

3 Does your best friend have to help at home a lot?
_____
_____

4 Do you have to do homework over the weekend?
_____
_____

should / shouldn't   → SB p.69

5 ★☆☆ **Circle the correct words.**

0 The film starts in 10 minutes. We're late, so we *should* / *shouldn't* hurry up.

1 Mum doesn't know when she'll be home, so she said we *should* / *shouldn't* wait for her to eat.

2 It's just a T-shirt. Why does it cost £65? It *should* / *shouldn't* be so expensive.

3 Why are you angry with me? You *should* / *shouldn't* try to understand me.

4 Tom needs to rest, so we *should* / *shouldn't* wake him up.

5 Juliet doesn't like her school uniform. She thinks students *should* / *shouldn't* wear what they want.

6 ★★☆ **Complete the conversations. Use** *should* **or** *shouldn't* **and a phrase from the list.**

> leave home earlier | ~~put on a jumper~~
> stay much longer | talk to her | worry so much

0 **A** I'm feeling cold.

    B I think you _should put on a jumper_ .

1 **A** I can't believe it. I'm late for school again!

    B Perhaps you _____ .

2 **A** I don't think Lily is very happy at all.

    B Maybe you _____ .

3 **A** I'm a bit nervous about my English test.

    B You _____ . It's not helpful.

4 **A** It's getting late.

    B Yes, I know. We _____ .

7 ★★★ **Answer the questions. Your answers can be funny or serious. Give reasons.**

0 Should children get money for helping at home?
Yes, they should, because parents get money for their work, too.

1 Should students get money for going to school?
_____

2 Should the Internet be free for everybody?
_____

3 Should every child have a tablet?
_____

mustn't / don't have to   → SB p.70

8 ★☆☆ **Look at the rules for a youth hostel. Circle the correct words.**

HOSTEL HOUSE RULES

- Last time for checkout: 11.30 am.
- Music? OK, but use headphones.
- Switch off lights at 10 pm!
- Breakfast 7.30 – 9.30 am.
- Please wash up after eating.
- Leave your shoes near the entrance.

0 You (mustn't)/ *don't have to* have the lights on after 10 pm.

1 You *mustn't / don't have to* leave dirty dishes in the kitchen.

2 You *mustn't / don't have to* play music out loud.

3 You *mustn't / don't have to* wear your shoes in the hostel.

4 You *mustn't / don't have to* check out before 10 o'clock.

5 You *mustn't / don't have to* have breakfast at 7.30.

9 ★★☆ **Match the sentences and complete them with** *mustn't* **or** *don't have to*.

0 My parents aren't very strict. ☐ *e*

1 Sarah hasn't got any problems with her work. ☐

2 The test will be hard. ☐

3 It's a secret. ☐

4 The doctor says Bea's fine. ☐

5 Thanks for Jamie's number. ☐

a You _____ help her.

b I _____ forget to call him.

c You _____ tell anyone.

d She _____ take medicine any longer.

e I _don't have to_ do much housework at home.

f You _____ forget to study every day now.

10 ★★★ **Answer the questions so they are true for you.**

1 What jobs do you have to do at home?
_____
_____

2 What are two things you mustn't do in your class?
_____
_____

3 Name three things you have to do during the week, but not on a Sunday.
_____
_____

4 What does your friend have to do that you don't have to do?
_____
_____

GET IT *RIGHT!*

have* (*got*) *to / don't have to / must / mustn't / should / shouldn't

We always use the base form of the verb after *have* **(***got***) *to / don't have to / must / mustn't / should / shouldn't*.**

✓ You **should ask** your sister to help you.

✗ You should ~~to~~ ask your sister to help you.

Circle **the correct words.**

1 You don't have *make / to make / making* dinner. We can order pizza.

2 That music is very loud. You should *use / to use / using* headphones.

3 You must *be / to be / being* careful. It's dark in the garden.

4 He shouldn't *worry / to worry / worrying* about the exam. He always gets good marks.

5 Tell Sarah she mustn't *forget / to forget / forgetting* to tidy her room.

6 What do I have *do / to do / doing* to join this club?

VOCABULARY
Gadgets

→ SB p.68

1 ★☆☆ **Complete the puzzle. What is the 'mystery word'?**

0 | C O F F E E M A C H I N E
1 |
2 |
3 |
P
4 |
5 |
6 |
7 |
8 |

0 Many people need it to make a drink for the breakfast (2 words).

1 An electronic gadget that allows you to store music in a special format and play it (2 words).

2 Drivers use it to find their way.

3 You need it when your hair is wet (2 words).

4 A small light you hold in your hand; it usually has a battery.

5 A gadget or phone app that's useful for Maths

6 The controls for a machine to play games (2 words).

7 A gadget that allows you to switch an electronic machine on or off from a distance (2 words).

8 A gadget that connects one piece of electronic equipment to another (2 words).

The mystery word is _____

Housework

→ SB p.71

2 ★☆☆ **Match the parts of the sentences.**

0 Luke's friends are staying for lunch. Can [f]
1 There are no clean plates left. Can you [ ]
2 I dropped some sugar on the floor. Will you [ ]
3 My room is a mess, but I'm too lazy [ ]
4 Can you do the cooking tonight? I did it [ ]
5 I'll do the washing, but I really don't want [ ]
6 We have no food left in the house. Can you [ ]
7 The dishwasher's full – I have to empty it [ ]
8 My mum showed me how to make my bed [ ]

a do the washing up quickly?
b yesterday, and the day before yesterday.
c to tidy it.
d when I was still a child.
e do the shopping if I tell you what we need?
f you set the table, please?
g before we can load it again.
h help me vacuum it?
i to do the ironing, too.

3 ★★★ **What housework do you like/dislike? Write four sentences about you.**

I don't like ironing clothes. I think it's boring.
I don't mind doing the cooking. It's ...
I hate ... . I think it's ...

_____
_____
_____
_____
_____
_____

WordWise: Expressions with *like*

→ SB p.69

4 ★☆☆ **Match the sentences with the pictures.**

0 Abbie's like her mum. They both love nature. [c]
1 It looks like a heart. [ ]
2 I think Dad's home. That sounds like his car! [ ]
3 It smells like an apple, but it doesn't look like one. [ ]

REFERENCE

Gadgets

calculator

coffee machine

docking station

games console

hair dryer

headphones

MP3 player

remote control

satnav

torch

Housework

do	load / empty	tidy up
the cooking	the dishwasher	the house
the ironing	**vacuum**	the room
the shopping	the carpet	**make**
the washing	the floor	the beds
the washing-up (wash up)	**set / clear**	
	the table	

VOCABULARY *EXTRA*

1 **Write the words under the photos.**

<del>camera</del> | keyboard | mouse | printer | screen | smartwatch

0

camera

1

_____

2

_____

3

_____

4

_____

5

_____

2 **Complete the lists.**

1 Electronic gadgets your family has at home: _____

2 The five gadgets you use most: _____

GADGETS FOR A BETTER WORLD

Professor Joshua Silver is a physicist at the University of Oxford. He also can't see very well! Joshua doesn't like buying new glasses when his eyes get worse. He had an idea to make glasses where you can change the strength of the lens. The glasses have liquid inside the plastic. To make the glasses stronger, you turn a wheel on each lens and this adds more liquid. If the glasses are too strong, you turn the wheel the other way, taking away some of the liquid. The liquid changes the shape of the lens. It's an incredibly useful invention, and it is also very cheap to make each pair of glasses.

Glasses that anyone can use, and that last forever, have the power to change people's lives. Joshua Silver is working to provide 1 billion pairs of his glasses to people around the world. This means that children can read their lessons at school and adults can continue to work and support their families.

Kenneth Shinozuka from New York City, US, lives with his parents and grandparents. Kenneth's grandfather has Alzheimer's, a disease that is common in old people. People with this illness often forget things and sometimes get lost. Kenneth's grandfather kept getting out of bed at night and walking around. One night, he left the house and his family were very worried because they didn't know where he was.

Kenneth wanted to do something to help his grandpa. What was his idea? A brilliant invention called SafeWander. Small discs go on the bottom of a normal pair of socks. When the person steps on the floor, the discs send a message to a smartphone and the phone rings an alarm. Kenneth tested the socks on his grandfather and they worked! Now his family don't have to watch Grandpa all night. He wears the socks and they know when he gets out of bed. Kenneth was only 15 when he made SafeWander and he won prizes for his invention. Now his 'smart socks' are helping other people like his grandfather to stay safe.

💬 8   ♡ 16   🔁 5

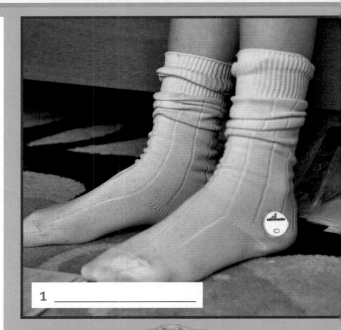

1 _____

2 _____

 **READING**

1   Read the article. Write the names of the inventors under the photos.

2   Read the article again. Mark the sentences T (true) or F (false). Correct the false sentences.

   0   Joshua Silver needs glasses. `T`
   1   With Joshua's glasses, people only need one pair. ☐
   2   He has sold a billion pairs of glasses. ☐
   3   Kenneth doesn't spend much time with his grandfather. ☐
   4   Kenneth's grandfather often got lost during the day. ☐
   5   Kenneth's invention helps people with Alzheimer's. ☐

3   **CRITICAL THINKING** Which of the gadgets in the article is the most useful? Why?

   _____
   _____
   _____

4   **CRITICAL THINKING** Complete the table with three gadgets that you use.

Name of gadget	What it helps you to do

DEVELOPING Writing

Taking notes and writing a short paragraph

1 **INPUT** Read the text. Tick (✓) the things that Alexander Graham Bell experimented with.

A famous INVENTOR

When Alexander Graham Bell was 29, he made one of the most important inventions in the history of the world: the telephone. A year later, he started the Bell Telephone Company. It became very successful. He became a businessman and earned a lot of money from his telephone company.

But Alexander Graham Bell wasn't only interested in money. He was interested in making inventions. He always wanted to learn and to try and create new things. He never stopped thinking of new ideas. He used his money to open laboratories with teams of engineers who could help him make his dreams come true.

Bell was also fascinated with propellers and kites and did lots of experiments with them. In 1907, four years after the Wright Brothers made their first flight, Bell formed the Aerial Experiment Association with four young engineers. Their plan was to build planes. The group was successful. Their plane named Silver Dart made the first successful flight in Canada on 23 February 1909.

 1

 2

 3

 4

 5

2 **ANALYSE** Look at a student's notes on the first paragraph of the text in Exercise 1. Underline the ideas in the text that the student used.

Alexander Graham Bell

1 29: invented telephone
2 30: started Bell Telephone Company — very successful
3 businessman — lots of money

3 **PLAN** Read the second and third paragraphs of the text again. Underline five important points and write them in the form of notes.

_____
_____
_____
_____
_____

✏️ WRITING TIP: making notes on a text

- Read the whole text for general understanding.
- Read each paragraph carefully and underline the important information.
- For each paragraph make short notes: just write words, not sentences, and leave out all unnecessary information.
- Make sure your notes are clear and include all the important information from each paragraph.

4 **PRODUCE** Write a paragraph to summarise the text about Alexander Graham Bell in 100–130 words using your notes from Exercises 2 and 3.

LISTENING

1 🔊 **7.01** **Listen to the conversations. For questions 1–3, choose the correct answers A, B or C.**

Conversation 1

1 What's the problem?

  A The camera doesn't work.

  B The USB cable isn't plugged in.

  C The laptop doesn't work.

Conversation 2

2 What does Daniel have to do?

  A tidy his room

  B walk the dog

  C wash up

Conversation 3

3 What did Evan borrow without asking?

  A a digital camera

  B an MP3 player

  C a laptop

2 🔊 **7.01** **Listen again. Complete the sentences from the conversations.**

Stella	Let ⁰ _me_ ¹s_____ . You ²h_____ ³t_____ switch ⁴y_____ ⁵c_____ on.
Daniel	All right. ⁶G_____ you. Do I ⁷h_____ to ⁸t_____ up my desk ⁹t_____ ?
Lily	Well, you ¹⁰m_____ use ¹¹m_____ ¹²th_____ without ¹³a_____ .

DIALOGUE

3 🔊 **7.02** **Complete the conversation with the expressions in the list.**

> do you mean | like what | sorry

Oliver	I want to do a mini-triathlon on Sunday.
Maya	¹_____ ?
Oliver	A mini-triathlon. That's three races in one.
Maya	Three races in one? What ²_____ ?
Oliver	Well, you have to swim 1 km, cycle 10 km, and run 3 km.
Maya	Really? That sounds like hard work. Why is it called mini?
Oliver	Because in a normal triathlon there are harder challenges.
Maya	³_____ ?
Oliver	Well, in the Olympic triathlon they swim 1.5 km, cycle 40 km, and run 10 km.
Maya	Wow! I think we should try the mini race!
Oliver	I think you're right.

4 **Write a short conversation for this picture. Use some of the expressions from Exercises 2 and 3.**

_____

_____

_____

_____

_____

_____

_____

_____

PHRASES FOR FLUENCY 　➔ SB p.72

5 🔊 **7.03** **Complete the conversation with the expressions in the list.**

> absolutely | all right | and stuff
> H̶e̶y̶ | never mind | no chance

Ada	⁰_____ _Hey_ _____ , Esma, what are you doing after school?
Esma	After school? Why?
Ada	I just want to know if you want to play basketball.
Esma	Basketball! ¹_____ , I've got to do housework ²_____ .
Ada	OK, ³_____ . So, what about tomorrow? Can we play then?
Esma	⁴_____ .
Ada	⁵_____ , see you then. Don't forget your basketball things!

> **PRONUNCIATION**
> Vowel sounds: /ʊ/ and /uː/ Go to page 120.

A2 Key for Schools

 READING AND WRITING
Part 1: 3-option multiple choice

1 **For each question, choose the correct answer.**

1

> **Please turn off the coffee machine at night and keep this area clean.**

What is this sign telling people to do?

A They must clean the coffee machine every night.

B They should turn off the coffee machine before they clean it.

C They must not leave the machine on during the night.

4

> No digital gadgets in the exam room.
>
> **PLEASE LEAVE HERE.**

A Students don't have to take their phones into the room.

B Students mustn't take their phones into the room.

C Students can't leave their phones here.

2

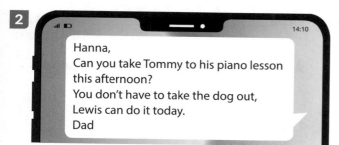

> Hanna,
> Can you take Tommy to his piano lesson this afternoon?
> You don't have to take the dog out, Lewis can do it today.
> Dad

A Hanna must take the dog for a walk.

B Hanna must ask Lewis to collect Tommy.

C Hanna has to go with Tommy to his lesson.

5

> **WARNING!**
>
> This toy has small parts. It is dangerous and **not** for children under 3.

A Children under three must be careful with this toy.

B This toy is for small children.

C Only children over three should use this toy.

3

> **WARNING!**
>
> Save and close your document. Then restart the computer.
>
> OK

A There is no problem with the computer.

B You should switch off and then switch on.

C You don't have to save your work.

6

> Joe,
> I'll be home late today, I'm going to an art class after work.
> Please start making dinner, but don't eat without me!
> Mum

A Mum will be back at the usual time.

B Joe must wait for his mum.

C Joe doesn't have to cook dinner.

EXAM GUIDE: READING AND WRITING PART 1

In A2 Key for Schools Reading and Writing Part 1, there are six short texts and you choose the option with the correct meaning. The texts are usually notices, signs, emails or text messages. There are three options and you choose one.

• Look at the context: Is it a message? A notice? Where would you see it?

• You won't always find the same words in the texts and sentences. Look for words and phrases with similar meanings.

• Often the sentences summarise the whole text but say it in a different way.

• Be careful when there are negative verbs.

• When you finish, read through your answers again to check they are right.

8 A QUESTION OF SPORT

Grammar rap!
▶23

ⓖ GRAMMAR
Past continuous

→ SB p.76

1 ★☆☆ **Complete the text with *was* or *were*.**

It was a cold winter's morning. It ⁰_____*was*_____ raining a little. Mums and dads ¹_____ standing by the school football field. They ²_____ chatting and drinking coffee to keep warm. They ³_____ waiting for the game to begin.

On the field, their daughters ⁴_____ getting ready for the big match. Some of them ⁵_____ running and others ⁶_____ kicking balls about. The goalkeeper ⁷_____ practising catching the ball.

Everyone was excited. It was the final of the under 16s girls' football tournament. Mr Fletcher, the headmaster, ⁸_____ cleaning his glasses. He put them on, took the whistle out of his pocket, and blew it.

2 ★★★ **Complete the text. Choose the correct words and write them in the correct form.**

clap | cry | hold | ~~jump~~ | not enjoy
not feel | sit | take | talk

I got there very late. The game was over. The girls of Blacon High School ⁰_____*were jumping*_____ up and down. They were the champions. Their proud parents ¹_____ .
One girl ²_____ up the trophy and showing it to the crowd and a journalist ³_____ lots of photos.
But not everyone was happy. The girls on the losing team ⁴_____ on the ground. Some of them had their heads in their hands and they ⁵_____ . They certainly ⁶_____ the celebrations.
Mr Fletcher ⁷_____ to them, but they ⁸_____ great.
Another year and still no trophy.

> **PRONUNCIATION**
> Strong and weak forms of *was* and *were*
> Go to page 120. 🎧

3 ★★☆ **Complete the sentences. Use the past continuous of the verbs in brackets.**

0 Phoebe _____*wasn't watching*_____ (not watch) TV, she _____*was playing*_____ (play) games.

1 I _____ (not play) tennis, I _____ (watch) a tennis match.

2 They _____ (not speak) Polish, they _____ (speak) Russian.

3 Our team _____ (not lose), we _____ (win).

4 Dad _____ (not swim), he _____ (sit) on the beach.

4 ★☆☆ **Match the questions with the answers.**

0 Were you listening to me? | d |

1 Was he laughing? | |

2 Was it raining? | |

3 Were they talking? | |

4 Was I sleeping? | |

5 Were we making a lot of noise? | |

a Yes, it was. We got really wet.

b Yes, they were, but I didn't hear what they said.

c Yes, I think you were.

d Yes, I heard everything you said.

e No, I don't think we were.

f No, he wasn't. He didn't think it was very funny.

5 ★★☆ **Answer the questions so they are true for you.**

What were you doing …

1 at 7 am today?

_____

2 at 6 pm yesterday?

_____

3 this time yesterday?

_____

4 at 10 o'clock last Sunday morning?

_____

Past continuous vs. past simple → SB p.79

6 ★☆☆ **Match the parts of the sentences.**

0 While the teacher was talking, [e]
1 Evan was making an omelette [ ]
2 The boys were fighting [ ]
3 We were staying in a youth hostel [ ]
4 While I was reading in the bath, [ ]
5 She was brushing her teeth [ ]

a when he burned his hand on the pan.
b when their mum walked into the room.
c I dropped my book in the water.
d but the toothbrush broke.
e I put my hand up to ask a question.
f when we met Sandro.

7 ★★☆ **Circle the correct words.**

0 Matthew *played* / *was playing* the guitar when he *fell* / *was falling* off the stage.
1 I *watched* / *was watching* a football match when my sister *came* / *was coming* into the room.
2 John and his sister *walked* / *were walking* to school when the accident *happened* / *was happening*.
3 I *talked* / *was talking* about Kiki when she *phoned* / *was phoning* me.
4 Alma *fell* / *was falling* and hurt her leg while she *skied* / *was skiing*.
5 While Ellie *studied* / *was studying*, she *remembered* / *was remembering* it was her mum's birthday.
6 Josh *lost* / *was losing* his phone while he *ran* / *was running*.

when and *while* → SB p.79

8 ★★☆ **Complete the sentences with *when* or *while*.**

0 ____*While*____ I was trying to get to sleep, the dog started barking.
1 She was eating an apple _____ she bit her tongue.
2 We were driving in the car _____ we saw Robin on his bike.
3 _____ I was waiting at the bus stop, I realised I didn't have any money.
4 Olivia was doing the Maths test _____ her phone rang.
5 _____ I was walking into town, I saw I had different socks on.

9 ★★★ **Write two sentences about each picture.**

0 Pablo / swim / saw / a turtle
While Pablo was swimming, he saw a turtle.
Pablo was swimming when he saw a turtle.

1 George / rock climb / drop / his bag
_____
_____

2 Megan / windsurf / fall / into the sea
_____
_____

3 Sasha and Eva / walk / in the mountains / they / got lost
_____
_____

GET IT RIGHT!

Past continuous

We form the past continuous with *was/were* + the *-ing* form of the verb. We use *was* with *I, he* and *she* and *were* with *we, you* and *they*.

✓ We were playing football when it started to rain.
✗ We ~~was playing~~ football when it started to rain.
✓ I was windsurfing when the accident happened.
✗ I ~~were windsurfing~~ when the accident happened.

Complete the sentences with *was* or *were*.

1 The rain started while they _____ having a picnic.
2 My friends and I _____ enjoying the competition when the TV stopped working.
3 My brother _____ winning the race when he fell off his bike.
4 _____ you driving when it started to snow?

VOCABULARY
Sports and sports verbs

→ SB p.76

1 ★★☆ Use the photos to find nine sports that fit into the word lines. The grey boxes contain the last letter of one word and the first letter of the next word.

					S												

			G							S						

			S					G		F						

There are four sports that don't fit into the word lines. What are they?

1 _____ 2 _____ 3 _____ 4 _____

2 ★★★ Circle the odd word out and explain why.

0 tennis   rugby   (windsurfing)   basketball
The other sports all use balls.

1 skiing   snowboarding   swimming   ski jumping
_____

2 windsurfing   rock climbing   sailing   diving
_____

3 tennis   rugby   volleyball   football
_____

Adverbs of sequence

→ SB p.79

3 ★★☆ Write sentences. Use the expressions in the list to start each sentence.

At first | After half an hour | Finally | Then

0 nervous
At first, I was nervous.

1 instructor / show / what to do
_____

2 could stand up
_____

3 ski / down the hill
_____

4 ★★★ Write a mini-story. Use the expressions and your own ideas.

The Tennis Game

1 At first …   3 After …
2 Then …   4 Finally …

REFERENCE
Sports

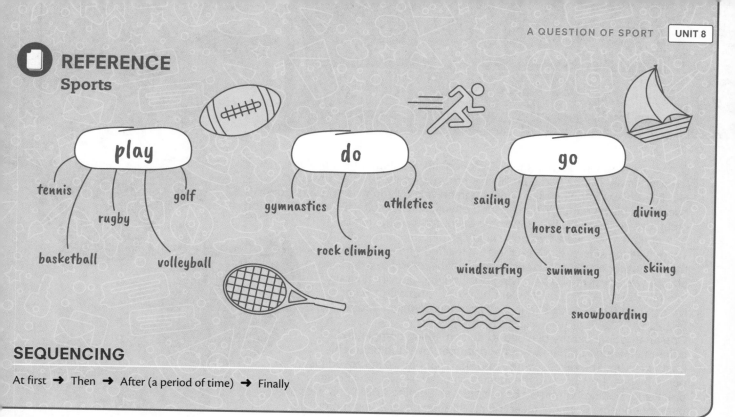

play	do	go
tennis	gymnastics	sailing
rugby	athletics	horse racing
golf	rock climbing	diving
basketball		windsurfing
volleyball		swimming
		skiing
		snowboarding

SEQUENCING

At first ➜ Then ➜ After (a period of time) ➜ Finally

VOCABULARY *EXTRA*

1 Write the words under the pictures.

badminton | baseball | ~~hockey~~
inline skating | surfing | table tennis

0 hockey

1

2

3

4

5

2 Complete the mind map with the names of sports.

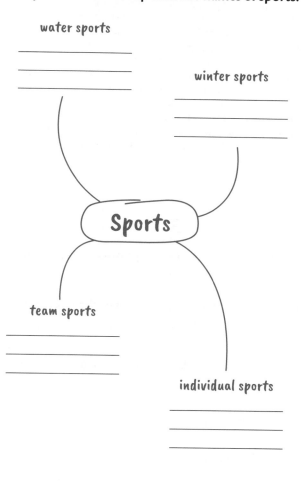

water sports
_____
_____
_____

winter sports
_____
_____

Sports

team sports
_____
_____
_____

individual sports
_____
_____
_____

People who changed sport: DICK FOSBURY

Like many American teenagers, Dick Fosbury wanted to be a professional sportsman, but he had a problem – he wasn't very good at any sport. He didn't play football well, and although he was tall, he wasn't a very good basketball player either. When he tried athletics, his results still weren't great, but he found that he had some talent for the high jump. At that time, there were two popular styles of jumping over the bar. There was *the scissors*, where the athlete lifted one leg first and then the other over the bar, and there was *the straddle*, where the athlete went over the bar in a lying position, face down. Fosbury used the straddle. The best height he could jump was 1.63 m. It wasn't bad, but it was a long way from the Olympic record of 2.23 m.

One afternoon, Fosbury decided to do something completely different. He took off backwards and jumped over the bar on his back, face up. The results were amazing. That day he improved his personal best by 15 cm. In the following years, he spent all his time practising, getting better and better. He was starting to win competitions, but most people were confused by his strange style. A year before the 1968 Olympics, he was the number 61 jumper in the world, and he was lucky to get into the US Olympic team.

When he arrived in Mexico, not many people knew his name. On the day of the high jump final, he walked on to the field with all the other jumpers. As the competition started, the 80,000 people in the crowd began to notice that one of the jumpers had a very strange style. At first they thought it was funny and laughed each time Fosbury jumped over the bar. After nearly four hours there were only three jumpers left. The crowd weren't laughing at Fosbury any more – they were cheering him on. The bar was at 2.24 m – a new Olympic record. The other two jumpers knocked it off but Fosbury flew over. The gold medal was his.

Dick Fosbury was now famous all over the world and his *Fosbury flop* changed forever the way that high jumpers jumped.

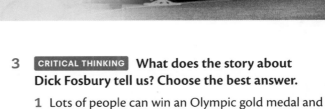

READING

1 Read the article. Match photos 1–3 with the names of the high jump styles in *italics*.

2 Read the article again. Answer the questions.

0 Why did Fosbury choose to do the high jump?
Because it was the only sport that he was good at.

1 How high could he jump on the day he invented his new style?
_____

2 What did people first think about his new style?
_____

3 How good was he at the high jump in 1967?
_____

4 Was he the favourite to win the gold medal in the Olympics? Explain your answer.
_____

5 How do people remember Dick Fosbury today?
_____

3 CRITICAL THINKING What does the story about Dick Fosbury tell us? Choose the best answer.

1 Lots of people can win an Olympic gold medal and break a world record.

2 Believe in yourself and don't let other people discourage you.

3 You must start a sport when you are a child to become a champion.

4 High jumping is a good choice for people who aren't very good at sport.

4 CRITICAL THINKING Why do you think Dick Fosbury was successful? Put the ideas in order of importance for you.

☐ He wanted to be a sports champion.
☐ His new way of jumping was very good.
☐ He trained and practised a lot.
☐ He didn't worry when people laughed at him.

An article

1 INPUT **Read the text. Where do you think it comes from?**

A A newspaper ☐   B A school magazine ☐   C A holiday website ☐   D A story book ☐

How I got into MOUNTAIN BIKING

By Caitlin Rogers

It was all because of my best friend, Zara. We were having lunch one day when ¹☐. I didn't have my own bike at that time, but Zara lent me her old one. We went to a forest that she knew very well and we got on our bikes. I was soon riding up and down the hills and it felt great! And guess what? ²☐. It's the same as riding a normal bike – you are just riding on paths instead of on the road.

I asked for a bike for my birthday ³☐. Now I ride every weekend. Sometimes we get a little wet and dirty, but I don't mind. ⁴☐. So, if you like doing exercise and being outside, maybe mountain biking is for you, too!

2 ANALYSE **Read the text again and complete it with the missing sentences. Write A–D in the gaps.**

A It's all part of the fun
B You don't have to go fast
C and then I joined the local club
D she invited me to go mountain biking with her

✎ WRITING TIP: an article

An article is a piece of writing in a newspaper, magazine or on a website.

- Think about your readers. Who are they? What are they interested in?
- You can use informal language in an article.
- You can speak to the readers directly. For example, you might want to ask a question or make a suggestion.
- Don't just write about facts. Describe what the experience was like and how you felt.
- Use some adjectives and adverbs to make your writing interesting.

3 PLAN **Choose ONE of these topics for an article and make notes in the plan.**

- A sports match between your school and another one
- A school trip
- How you started a new sport

TITLE: _____

PARAGRAPH 1: Set up the situation (e.g. time, place).
_____
_____

PARAGRAPH 2: Describe what happened.
_____
_____

PARAGRAPH 3: Describe how the situation ended and/or give your opinion.
_____
_____

4 PRODUCE **Write your article for a school magazine (about 120–140 words). Use your notes from Exercise 3.**

🎧 LISTENING

1 🔊 **8.02** Listen to the street interviews. Who does, or wants to do, these sports, the girl (G) or the boy (B)?

0 G 3 ☐ 6 ☐

1 ☐ 4 ☐ 7 ☐

2 ☐ 5 ☐ 8 ☐

2 🔊 **8.02** Listen again. Mark the sentences T (true) or F (false).

0 The girl thinks the sports centre looks good. [T]

1 The girl isn't very interested in sport. ☐

2 You can do water sports at the sports centre. ☐

3 The boy thinks the sports centre cost too much. ☐

4 The sports centre has a skating track. ☐

DIALOGUE

3 Put the words in order to make questions and answers.

0 of / sports / do / think / What / centre? / you / the / new
What do you think of the new sports centre?

1 brilliant / think / I / it's
_____

2 sports / do / feel / you / centre? / How / the / about / new
_____

3 money / of / I / a / waste / it's / think
_____

4 🔊 **8.03** Put the sentences in order to make a conversation.

A ☐ Well, we need a new swimming pool.

A ☐ I don't agree.

A [1] What do you think of the new library?

A ☐ I think it's a waste of money. There are better things to spend our money on.

B ☐ For example?

B ☐ I like it. I think it's really good for our town.

B ☐ So how do you feel about it, then?

B ☐ I'm sorry, but I think a library is more important than a swimming pool.

Train to TH!NK

Sequencing

5 Which sequence (A–E) do these words belong to and where should they go?

0 afternoon [C] *between morning and evening*

1 baby ☐ _____

2 today ☐ _____

3 Saturday ☐ _____

4 wake up ☐ _____

A	child teenager adult
B	Monday Wednesday Friday
C	morning evening night
D	go to school have lunch come home
E	yesterday tomorrow next weekend

6 Put the lists of words in order. Add one more item at the end of each list.

0 October / March / June
March, June, October, (November)

1 third / second / fourth
_____

2 get into the water / go to the sports centre / go to the pool
_____

3 sometimes / often / rarely
_____

A2 Key for Schools

🎧 LISTENING
Part 2: Gap fill

1 🔊 **8.04** **For each question, write the correct answer in the gap. Write one word, or a number, or a date or a time.**

You will hear a girl talking about her football team.

Name: Boxton United Girls' Football Club
Training day: ¹_____
Kit: Yellow shirt and ²_____ shorts
Cost: ³_____ a month
Training: at the park in ⁴_____ Road
Contact Becky on: ⁵_____

EXAM GUIDE: LISTENING PART 2

In A2 Key for Schools Listening Part 2, you listen to one person speaking and complete some notes.

- Before you listen, read the title and the notes carefully because they give you an idea about what you are going to hear.
- Focus on the gaps and try to imagine what sort of information you need to listen for – for example, a date, a price, a number or a word.
- You will hear the missing information in the same order as the notes.
- Use the first listening to write in as many of the answers as you can. Use the second listening to check these answers and complete the other gaps.

2 🔊 **8.05** **For each question, write the correct answer in each gap. Write one word, or a number, or a date or a time. You will hear a boy talking about the Olympic Stadium in Rio de Janeiro.**

- Name: The Maracanã Stadium
- Distance from Copacabana beach: ¹_____ km
- Opened in ²_____ 1950
- The 1950 FIFA World Cup winners were: ³_____
- The Olympic and Paralympic games took place here in ⁴_____
- Stadium used for: football and ⁵_____

🎧 LISTENING
Part 4: 3-option multiple choice

EXAM GUIDE: LISTENING PART 4

In A2 Key for Schools Listening Part 4, you listen to five short dialogues and monologues and then choose the correct answer A, B or C.

- Before you listen, read the questions and the three options.
- You hear each dialogue or monologue twice.
- The questions are not usually about details or facts. You need to identify the main point, idea, message or the gist of what you hear.
- When you listen, focus on general understanding and listen for key words.
- Don't choose an answer just because you hear the same word in the listening. Listen carefully to what the speakers say about it.

3 🔊 **8.06** **For each question, choose the correct answer.**

1 You will hear two friends talking about a football match. Why does the boy feel upset?
   A They played badly.
   B His team were lucky.
   C They lost the match.

2 You will hear a sports teacher giving instructions to her class. Which sport are they playing?
   A basketball
   B tennis
   C football

3 You will hear a sports report on the radio. Which country won the competition?
   A Australia
   B the US
   C Canada

4 You will hear two friends talking. Where did the accident happen?
   A in the mountains
   B in the hotel
   C in a ski lesson

5 You will hear two friends talking about a competition. How does Ellie feel?
   A happy
   B sad
   C worried

CONSOLIDATION

🎧 LISTENING

1 🔊 **8.07** **Listen to the conversation. Choose the correct answer A, B or C.**

1 What lesson has Lucy got at the sports centre today?
  A gym
  B rock climbing
  C swimming

2 What is in the bathroom?
  A a hair dryer
  B a tablet
  C headphones

3 What is on the living room floor?
  A magazines
  B a games console
  C a docking station

2 🔊 **8.07** **Listen again and answer the questions.**

0 How long is it until Lucy's lesson starts?
  Two hours.

1 Why does she want to go to the sports centre early?
  _____
  _____

2 What does her dad want her to do?
  _____
  _____

3 What was Lucy's dad doing when he sat on the headphones?
  _____
  _____

4 Where is Lucy's tablet?
  _____
  _____

5 Where does Lucy's dad want her to help him?
  _____
  _____

6 Why does he think cutting wood is a good idea for Lucy?
  _____
  _____

🔤 VOCABULARY

3 **Unscramble the letters and write the words.**

0 I'd love to go *nagilis*, but I can't swim and I'm scared I might fall in the water. ___*sailing*___

1 We don't all want to listen to your music. Put your *oehadpenhs* on. _____

2 I can't do this sum. Can I use the *alaclutocr* on your phone? _____

3 I tried to play *fogl* once, but I couldn't even hit the ball. _____

4 It's dark. I can't see anything. Have you got a *corth*? _____

ⓖ GRAMMAR

4 **Complete the sentences with the correct form of the verbs.**

0 They ___*had*___ (have) the accident while they ___*were programming*___ (program) the satnav.

1 I _____ (tidy) up my bedroom when I _____ (find) my torch.

2 She _____ (use) the coffee maker when she _____ (burn) her hand.

3 Dad _____ (tell) us to do our homework when we _____ (play) on the games console.

4 I _____ (listen) to music on my phone when it _____ (stop) working.

5 Ⓒircle the correct words.

Dad Hey, Max, why are you looking so sad?

Max We lost the match.

Dad You ⁰(*shouldn't*)/ *must* worry so much. You ¹*mustn't always* / *don't always* have to win.

Max Yes, but we never win. We ²*should* / *don't have to* try to win sometimes. Our coach says we ³*shouldn't* / *must* try harder. He thinks we ⁴*should* / *mustn't* have extra training sessions.

Dad What! You already have three. I think I ⁵*should* / *mustn't* have a chat with him.

Max It's OK, Dad. You ⁶*mustn't* / *don't have to* do that. I don't think I want to play for the team any more.

Dad Come on, Max, you ⁷*shouldn't* / *must* give up so easily.

Max But you always say that we ⁸*should* / *don't have to* love what we do. I don't even like playing football.

Dad Well, you ⁹*must* / *shouldn't* always listen to what I say. Sometimes even I get it wrong.

DIALOGUE

6 🔊 8.08 **Complete the conversation with the words in the list.**

> doing | fear | mean | ~~should~~ | skiing | sorry | sport | tell | what | windsurfing

Amy I'm bored.

Leo You ⁰___*should*___ get a hobby, then.

Amy Like ¹_____ ?

Leo Well, maybe you could start doing a
²_____ .

Amy You ³_____ do some exercise?

Leo Exactly. What about a water sport? Sailing or
⁴_____ , or something like that.

Amy But I've got aquaphobia – you know, a fear of water.

Leo OK, what about rock climbing? They do lessons at the gym.

Amy No, I've got acrophobia.

Leo ⁵_____ ?

Amy Acrophobia – it's a ⁶_____ of heights.

Leo Snowboarding? ⁷_____ ?

Amy No, I've got chionophobia.

Leo Don't ⁸_____ me – a fear of snow.

Amy Exactly.

Leo I think you've got lazyitis.

Amy What's that?

Leo The fear of ⁹_____ exercise!

📖 READING

7 **Read the text. Match the headings with the paragraphs.**

0 The prizes ☐ C

1 The places ☐

2 Try saying this! ☐

3 Young and old ☐

✏️ WRITING

8 **Choose a sport or a sportsperson that you like. Write a text called 'All you need to know about … ' (about 150 words).**

- Research some interesting facts and trivia.
- Organise your text into three or four short paragraphs.
- Try to write exactly 150 words.

ALL YOU NEED TO KNOW ABOUT THE
OLYMPIC GAMES IN 150 WORDS

A London is the only city to hold the Games three times (in 1908, 1948 and 2012). The US held them four times but in three different cities.

B At the Paris Games in 1900, there were more athletes than spectators. The oldest athlete ever at the games was Sweden's Oscar Swahn. He won a silver medal in shooting in 1920 at the age of 72. The youngest medal winner was Inge Sorensen from Denmark. She was 12 when she won a bronze medal in swimming.

C In the first modern Olympic Games, in Athens in 1896, there were no gold medals. The winners all got silver medals. In the 1900 Games, the winners got trophies instead of medals. Winners first got gold medals in the 1904 Olympics in St Louis, US.

D And finally, the longest name for an Olympic champion was Prapawadee Jaroenrattanatarakoon from Thailand. She won a gold medal in weightlifting.

9 WILD AND WONDERFUL

▶26 Grammar rap!

Ⓖ GRAMMAR
Comparative adjectives → SB p.86

1 ★☆☆ **Write the comparative form of the adjectives.**

0 old *older*
1 bad _____
2 beautiful _____
3 easy _____
4 expensive _____
5 good _____
6 happy _____
7 interesting _____
8 nice _____
9 young _____

2 ★★☆ **Complete sentence B with the comparative form of the adjective in A.**

0 **A** Question number 1 is difficult.
   B Yes, it is – but question number 2 is
   _____*more difficult*_____ !

1 **A** Was your laptop expensive?
   B Yes, it was, but the old one was
   _____ .

2 **A** She's young.
   B Yes, but her sister's _____
   than her.

3 **A** This book's interesting.
   B You're right, but the other one is
   _____ .

4 **A** Wow – that's a good bike!
   B It's not bad. Actually, I want to buy a
   _____ one than this!

5 **A** This film's bad!
   B Yes, but the other one was
   _____ !

3 ★★☆ **Complete the sentences. Use the comparative form of the adjectives.**

	Siena	Justine
Age:	12	13
Height:	1.58	1.56
Does homework:	sometimes	always
English score:	93%	74%

0 Siena is __*younger than*__ Justine. (young)
1 Siena is _____ Justine. (tall)
2 Justine is _____ Siena. (hard-working)
3 Siena is _____ at English
   _____ Justine. (good)

4 ★★★ **Write comparative sentences using your own ideas. Use the words in brackets to help you.**

1 your school / another school in your town (*big / good* ...?)
   _____

2 you / your best friend (*old / tall / intelligent* ...?)
   _____

3 two video games (*easy / enjoyable / exciting* ...?)
   _____

4 (any two things you want to compare)
   _____

can / can't for ability → SB p.87

5 ★☆☆ **Complete the sentences. Use *can* or *can't*.**

0 She ____*can ride.*____   2 She _____

1 He _____   3 He _____

6 ★★☆ **Complete the sentences using *can ... but ... can't ....* Think about sports, languages, music, cooking, art, etc.**

0 I ____*can sing, but I can't play any instruments.*
1 My best friend _____
2 My mum / dad _____
3 Babies _____
4 Dogs _____
5 I _____

Superlative adjectives
→ SB p.88

7 ★☆☆ **Complete the conversations.**

the best | ~~the laziest~~ | the most difficult
the most expensive | the most interesting
the oldest | the worst

0 A Who's _____the laziest_____ kid in your class?
   B Yuri. He never does anything!
1 A That test was hard!
   B It was. In fact it was _____ test this year.
2 A Do you think they're a good band?
   B Yes, I do. They're _____ band around at the moment.
3 A That's a great shirt.
   B Yes, it's really nice. But I can't buy it. It's _____ shirt in the shop!
4 A What a horrible day. Rain, rain, rain.
   B Yes, I think it's _____ day of the summer.
5 A Who's _____ person in your family?
   B Grandpa. He's 74.
6 A You really like History, don't you?
   B Yes, I think it's _____ subject at school.

8 ★★☆ **Complete the sentences with the superlative form of the adjectives in the list.**

boring | delicious | fast | high
important | ~~rich~~ | strong

0 She's got a really big house and a Porsche. She's _____the richest_____ person I know!
1 He can pick up a 50 kilo bag of potatoes. He's _____ man I know.
2 I almost fell asleep during the film. It was _____ film ever!
3 Let's have an ice cream here. It's _____ ice cream in town!
4 This car does 280 kph. Maybe it's _____ car in the world.
5 Which is _____ mountain in the world?
6 Some people say that the day you get married is _____ day of your life.

9 ★★☆ Ⓒircle the correct words.

0 Is the Amazon *longer* / ⓛthe longest river in the world?
1 Alex is *taller* / *the tallest* than me.
2 Yesterday was *colder* / *the coldest* day of the year.
3 My father is *younger* / *the youngest* than my mother.
4 He wants to be *richer* / *the richest* person in the country.
5 Is this exercise *easier* / *the easiest* one on this page?

10 ★★★ **Write one comparative sentence and one superlative sentence about the things in each group. Use the adjectives in the list to help you.**

big | boring | cheap | ~~cold~~ | delicious,
difficult | enjoyable | fast | good | healthy
~~hot~~ | interesting

0 winter – summer – autumn
   Summer is hotter than autumn.
   Winter's the coldest time of the year.
1 running – football – swimming
   _____
   _____
2 pizza – chips – salad
   _____
   _____
3 video games – films – books
   _____
   _____
4 Brazil – China – Britain
   _____
   _____
5 train – plane – bus
   _____
   _____

GET IT *RIGHT!*
Comparative and superlative adjectives

We form the comparative of <u>long</u> adjectives with *more* + adjective. We form the comparative of <u>short</u> adjectives (one syllable) with adjective + *-er*. Don't use *more* with adjective + *-er*.
✓ My cousin is **younger** than me.
✗ My cousin is ~~more younger~~ than me.
We form the superlative of long adjectives with *the most* + adjective. We form the superlative of short adjectives (one syllable) with *the* + adjective + *-est*. Don't use *the most* with short adjective + *-est*.
✓ It was **the coldest** winter in history.
✗ It was the ~~most coldest~~ winter in history.
Complete the text with the comparative or superlative form of the adjectives in brackets.
I love climbing mountains. For me, it's ¹_____ (exciting) hobby. I think ²_____ (beautiful) mountains in the world are in New Zealand. But ³_____ (tall) mountains in the world are in Asia. The mountains in Britain are ⁴_____ (low) than in Asia and the weather is ⁵_____ (wet). The US has ⁶_____ (warm) weather than Britain, but Asia's weather is ⁷_____ (hot).
So I love going climbing in Asia.

VOCABULARY
Geographical features → SB p.86

1 ★★☆ **Match the words a–j with the definitions 1–9.**

0 a place with lots of trees growing together `a`
1 an area of sand or rocks near the sea ☐
2 land with water all round it ☐
3 high land but not as high as a mountain ☐
4 water that moves across the land and into the sea ☐
5 very high land, sometimes with snow on top ☐
6 a big area of water with land around it ☐
7 a very large area of sea water ☐
8 a hot, humid forest with lots of tropical plants and animals ☐
9 a big, hot, dry area of land, often with sand ☐

a forest	f jungle
b island	g ocean
c hill	h river
d desert	i lake
e beach	j mountain

2 ★★★ **Complete the sentences with the words in Exercise 1.**

0 It's important to take lots of water with you if you go into the ___desert___ .
1 Madagascar is a very big _____ in the Indian Ocean.
2 I love sitting on a _____ and swimming in the sea.
3 The longest _____ in the world is the Nile.
4 Mount Everest is the highest _____ in the world.
5 I was very tired after I cycled up the _____ .
6 Let's go for a walk in the _____ and look for wild mushrooms!
7 We sailed round the _____ in a small boat.
8 Tigers live in the _____ in India and Indonesia.
9 The ship hit a rock and went to the bottom of the _____ .

The weather → SB p.89

3 ★☆☆ **Complete the 'weather' words with the missing letters.**

1 Yesterday was c _o_ _l_ _d_ , but today it's really f _ _ _zin_ _ ! It's a bit w_ _ _ _y, too.
2 It was nice and w_ _ _ _ yesterday. But today is even better: it's s_ _ _ ny, h_ _t and d_ _y!
3 It's a horrible day today. It's c_ _ _ _dy and cold. This morning it was r_ _ _ _y, so it's w_ _t here, too.
4 When it's f_ _ _ _ _ like today, it's hard to see where you're going!

4 **Complete the text with words from Exercise 3.**

I'm from Britain but I live in Brasilia, the capital of Brazil. The weather here is usually good – the temperature is normally between about 12° and 28°C, so it's never really [0]___cold___ . Sometimes in summer it's really [1]h_____ , but a lot of the time it's just nice and [2]w_____ , especially in the evenings.

There is one period in the year – from about May to July or August – when it rarely rains. So everything is very [3]d_____ . At other times of the year, the weather can be [4]r_____ and when it rains, it rains really hard!

Some days in the morning, when you wake up, the sky is grey and [5]c_____ , but then the clouds go away and the morning can be bright and [6]s_____ .

So, the weather here is quite nice, really – not like my home country, Britain, where it's often [7]f_____ in winter! I haven't seen ice here.

WordWise: Phrases with *with* → SB p.87

5 ★☆☆ **Complete the sentences with the phrases in the list.**

> busy with | good with | to do with
> with tomato sauce | with you
> ~~with 220 bedrooms~~

0 It's a big hotel _with 220 bedrooms_ .
1 **A** Isn't Alice here?
  B No. I thought she came _____ .
2 It's delicious – pasta _____ and chicken.
3 She looks after my little brother. She's really _____ children.
4 Please don't ask me about it. It's got nothing _____ you.
5 I phoned him but he didn't answer. He was _____ his homework.

REFERENCE

THE WEATHER

cloudy dry freezing humid 100% sunny wet

cold foggy hot rainy warm windy

GEOGRAPHICAL FEATURES

beach   desert   forest   hill   island   jungle   lake   mountain   ocean   river

PHRASES WITH *WITH*

be with someone

be busy with something

be good with (animals / children ...)

something / someone with (big windows / chocolate sauce / long hair ...)

It's got nothing to do with (you / me / us ...)

VOCABULARY *EXTRA*

1 Write the words under the photos.

cave | cliff | countryside | grass | pond | trees

0 _____*cliff*_____

1 _____

2 _____

3 _____

4 _____

5 _____

2 Where can you find the things below where you live?

0 grass _____*the football field*_____

1 cave _____

2 cliffs _____

3 pond _____

4 countryside _____

5 trees _____

85

POLE to POLE

1 **Read the article and label each photo with the name of the place: *The Arctic* or *Antarctica*.**

1 _____

The Arctic and Antarctica are some of the wildest and most interesting places on Earth. Scientists study them because they can help us understand the history of our planet and the effects of climate change.

So, what do you know about the Arctic and Antarctica? Most people know that they are very cold and icy, but not many people know about the differences between them.

The Arctic is in the north and the Antarctic is in the south. There are around 4 million people who live in the Arctic, but no one lives in Antarctica all the time. There's more than just snow and ice to see in both places. There are beautiful wild landscapes and some very special animals. However, polar bears and penguins don't live in the same place – so forget what you see in cartoons! In the sea around both places you can see seals, whales and fish.

2 _____

4 _____

And what about the weather? It's certainly freezing cold, but here's a surprise: a few parts of the Arctic and most of Antarctica get almost no rain or snow, so they are among the driest places on Earth. Antarctica is actually the world's largest desert!

More facts about these unusual places:

The Arctic	Antarctica
Climate **Average temperature** North Pole: 0°C – -40°C **Wind** Strong winds	**Climate** **Average temperature** South Pole: -28°C – -60°C **Wind** Windiest place on Earth
Landscape **Ice** (up to 5 m thick) + snow **Mountains** (highest: 3,694 m) Also grass, lakes, rivers – not many trees	**Landscape** **Ice** (up to 4.7 km thick) + snow **Mountains** (highest: 4,892 m) A few very small plants – no grass or trees
Animals Polar bears, seals, whales, fish, reindeer, foxes, wolves	**Animals** Penguins, seals, whales, fish
21 June Summer: 24 hrs light **21 December Winter:** 24 hrs dark	**21 June Winter:** 24 hrs dark **21 December Summer:** 24 hrs light

3 _____

2 **Read the first part of the text and mark the sentences T (true) or F (false). Correct the false sentences.**

1 Scientists think Antarctica is more interesting than the Arctic. ☐

2 More people live in the Arctic than in Antarctica. ☐

3 The same animals live in both places. ☐

4 There are penguins in the Arctic. ☐

5 Antarctica is the world's largest desert. ☐

3 **Read the information in the table and complete the sentences with *the Arctic* or *Antarctica*.**

0 ___*The Arctic*___ is warmer than ___*Antarctica*___ .

1 _____ is the coldest place on Earth.

2 _____ is windier than _____ .

3 The ice in _____ is thinner than in _____ .

4 _____ has got higher mountains than _____ .

5 Plants are rarer in _____ than in _____ .

6 There are more land animals in _____ than in _____ .

7 21 June is lighter in _____ than in _____ .

4 **CRITICAL THINKING** **What is the purpose of this text? Choose the correct answer.**

A To compare the Arctic and Antarctica.

B To talk about the animals that live in the North Pole.

C To explain why scientists are interested in the Arctic and Antarctica.

5 **What do you think? Tick the sentences you agree with and explain why.**

1 We must protect wild places on the planet. ☐

_____

2 We need to act quickly to stop climate change. ☐

_____

3 The Arctic and Antarctica are good places to live. ☐

_____

4 It's important to learn about animals in danger. ☐

_____

An email about a place

1 | INPUT | **Read Jake's email to Monika and answer the questions.**

1 Where is Monika going on holiday?

2 Which two places does Jake recommend?

Monika
Monika@thinkmail.com

Hey Monika,

So, you're going to South Korea? Lucky you! I went to South Korea two years ago with my family. It's a great place and I enjoyed it a lot. The food, the people, the places – so different from my country!

Anyway, I'm writing to give you some ideas. People usually arrive in Seoul and stay there for a few days. So when you're in Seoul, don't miss the Gyeongbokgung Palace! It's just fabulous. Here's a photo I took. You have to go there!

I know you like beaches and swimming so make sure you go to Jeju Island. It's in the south and you can swim, go diving and see lots of wonderful fish. It's very beautiful there.

Also, don't forget to listen to the music! K-pop's the best!

Sorry, I must go now – but just write if you want any more ideas!

Have a great holiday!

Jake

---

2 | ANALYSE | **Read Jake's email again. <u>Underline</u> the adjectives that he uses to give his opinion of things in South Korea.**

1 Are the adjectives positive or negative?

_____

2 Does Jake use any adjectives that are new for you? Look them up in a dictionary if you need to.

3 **Complete the phrases that Jake uses.**

0 _____*Don't miss*_____ Gyeongbokgung Palace.

1 You _____ go there!

2 _____ you go to Jeju Island.

3 _____ to listen to the music.

4 **What is Jake doing when he writes the sentences in Exercise 3?**

A Recommending / giving advice ☐

B Giving directions ☐

C Giving an opinion ☐

✎ **WRITING TIP: an informal email**

- Organise the information into paragraphs.
- Use informal phrases. (*Lucky you! It's just fabulous! The food/music/weather is the best!*)
- Begin and end with a friendly phrase. (*Hi, Hey / Have fun, Write soon, See you soon, Have a great time/holiday!*)

5 | PLAN | **You want to tell an English-speaking friend about a place that you know and like. Make notes about:**

- why the place is special

_____

_____

- some adjectives you can use to describe it

_____

_____

- the best places to visit

_____

_____

- the most exciting things to do

_____

_____

6 | PRODUCE | **Write your email to your friend in 120–140 words. Use Jake's email to help you.**

🎧 LISTENING

1 🔊 9.04 **Listen to the conversations. Mark the sentences T (true) or F (false).**

Conversation 1

0 The girl wants to go to the beach. ☐ F

1 The girl doesn't know what a jigsaw puzzle is. ☐

2 The girl doesn't want to do a jigsaw puzzle. ☐

3 It's raining. ☐

Conversation 2

4 It's a cloudy day. ☐

5 The boy doesn't want to wear trousers. ☐

6 The boy likes the girl's T-shirt. ☐

7 The girl doesn't understand the words on her T-shirt. ☐

2 🔊 9.04 **Listen again. Complete the lines from the conversations.**

Conversation 1

Boy What a ⁰___horrible___ day today.

Girl Yes, it ¹_____ .

Boy I just thought, well, something different, ²_____ a jigsaw puzzle.

Girl What a ³_____ ! On a rainy day like today, it's a nice thing to do!

Conversation 2

Boy Wow, ⁴_____ fantastic day. It's so warm and ⁵_____ !

Girl So let's ⁶_____ somewhere.

Girl Hey, nice shorts. They ⁷_____ cool.

Boy Thanks. And I really like your T-shirt – what a ⁸_____ colour!

DIALOGUE

3 🔊 9.05 **Complete the conversation with the words in the list.**

can | can't | idea | let's | maybe | perhaps

Boy What a horrible day. It's cold and snowing.

Girl I know. What ⁰___can___ we do?

Boy Well, we ¹_____ go outside. So, ²_____ do something here.

Girl Well, ³_____ we can watch a film.

Boy Well, OK, yes. Or ⁴_____ we could play some video games.

Girl That's a good ⁵_____ .

4 **Write a conversation for this picture. Use some of the expressions in Exercises 2 and 3.**

Park?

Wow, new bike.

_____

_____

_____

_____

_____

_____

PHRASES FOR FLUENCY → SB p.90

5 🔊 9.06 **Put the conversation in order. Then listen and check.**

☐ **A** No problem. I'll call Jenny in a minute, she'll probably know.

☐ **A** Oh, yes, that's fixed it! Well done. Thank you!

☐1 **A** Can you help me with my laptop? Something's wrong with it, and I don't know much about laptops.

☐ **A** Oh! So you can't help me, then?

☐ **B** Not really. I'm sorry.

☐ **B** Good idea. She's really good with these things. Oh – hang on! How about if you press this button here?

☐ **B** I don't know much either.

6 **Complete the phone conversation. Use the phrases in the list.**

either | ~~in a minute~~
no problem | not really | then

A Hi, John? Sorry, I'm a bit late. But I'll be at your place ⁰___in a minute___ .

B ¹_____ , Max. Is there a lot of traffic, ²_____ ?

A ³_____ . But I'm cycling and it's raining.

B Ugh. I hate cycling in the rain!

A I don't really like it ⁴_____ . But I haven't got any money for the bus. Anyway, I shouldn't really be cycling and talking on the phone at the same time. Bye!

A2 Key for Schools

 READING AND WRITING

Part 4: 3-option multiple-choice cloze

1 For each question, choose the correct answer.

Alice Springs

Alice Springs is in Australia. The town is in the centre of the country. About 24,000 people live there, and it is the ¹ … town in the area. It is 1500 km away from the cities of Adelaide and Darwin. The area ² … the town is a desert. It is very dry with red ³ … and rocks. Outside Alice Springs, there are mountains, and Uluru is not ⁴ … away. Uluru is a large and famous red rock that looks like it changes colour at different times of the day. The weather in Alice Springs is very hot, and it doesn't rain very much. In summer, the temperatures can be ⁵ … , around 36°C, and the winters are ⁶ … at around 20°C.

1 A biggest	B bigger	C big
2 A around	B inside	C between
3 A sea	B island	C sand
4 A close	B far	C near
5 A high	B higher	C highest
6 A freezing	B warm	C foggy

EXAM GUIDE: READING AND WRITING PART 4

In A2 Key for Schools Reading and Writing Part 4, you have to choose one word to complete each gap. This exercise tests your understanding of words in context.

- First, read the text without worrying about the gaps. It's important to know what the text is about before you start the exercise.

- Some of the gaps test vocabulary, so you have to choose the word with the right meaning. Re-read the sentence before and after the gap to help you decide.

- Other gaps are about grammar, so re-read the sentence with the gap and try each of the options to see which sounds best.

- Always choose one of the words. Never leave a blank space.

2 Read the email about Niagara Falls. Choose the correct word (A, B or C) for each gap.

Here we are at Niagara Falls!

It's one of the ¹ … amazing places in the world. There are three waterfalls here on the border between the US and Canada.

It's a fantastic place. However, Niagara Falls isn't ² … highest waterfall in the world (that's the Angel Falls in Venezuela), but it is very big. When you are close to it, the noise from the water is so ³ … you can't hear other people talking!

It's one of the most ⁴ … places to visit in North America with over 30 million visitors a year. There are lots of ways to see the falls. The ⁵ … way to get close is by boat. Visitors can also get a great ⁶ … of the falls from an island in the Niagara River.

1 A more	B much	C most
2 A than	B the	C a
3 A loud	B big	C high
4 A dangerous	B popular	C exciting
5 A best	B first	C good
6 A visit	B view	C experience

10 OUT AND ABOUT

⊙ GRAMMAR

be going to for intentions ⟶ SB p.94

1 ★☆☆ **Complete the sentences with the verb**
   to be. **Use short forms.**

   0 We ___'re___ going to see a show at the concert hall.
   1 I _____ going to buy some sun cream at the chemist's.
   2 They _____ going to the sports centre to play tennis.
   3 We _____ going to have lunch at the shopping mall.
   4 Taylor _____ going to catch the bus home.

2 ★★☆ **Complete the questions. Then match**
   them with the answers.

   0 ___Are___ you going ___to watch___
     the game? (watch) ☐ e

   1 _____ they going _____
     in a hotel? (stay) ☐

   2 _____ we going _____
     Gran this weekend? (visit) ☐

   3 _____ Daniel going _____
     a taxi? (take) ☐

   4 _____ Jo going _____
     the competition? (enter) ☐

   5 _____ Andrés going _____
     tonight? (cook) ☐

   a No, they aren't. They're going camping.
   b No, he's going to walk there.
   c Yes, she is. She says she's feeling lucky.
   d I hope so. He's really good at it.
   e Yes, I am. I love football.
   f Yes, we are. We're going to go on Sunday.

3 ★★☆ **Complete the answers with *going to* and**
   the verbs in brackets.

   What ⁰ ___are you going to do___ (do) when you
   leave school?

   A 'I ¹_____ (study) Maths
     at Nottingham University. Two of my friends
     ²_____ (go) there too, so we
     ³_____ (find) a house to rent.'

   B 'I'm not sure. My best friend
     ⁴_____ (travel) around
     the world, and he wants me to go with
     him. I ⁵_____ (not do)
     that – I haven't got enough money – but
     I ⁶_____ (not go) to
     university either.'

4 ★★★ **Write five plans you have for this year.**
   Use *going to*.

   I'm going to ... _____
   _____
   _____
   _____
   _____

Present continuous for arrangements ⟶ SB p.95

5 ★★☆ **Look at Claire's diary. Complete the**
   sentences with the present continuous of the verbs.

	MORNING	AFTERNOON	EVENING
MONDAY		tennis – Sue	kids – cinema
TUESDAY	breakfast with Tom		
WEDNESDAY			party at Nicole's
THURSDAY	meeting with Jen	dentist – 4 pm	
FRIDAY	golf		fly to Rome

   0 Claire and Sue ___are playing___ (play)
     tennis on Monday afternoon.
   1 Claire _____ (fly) to Rome on
     Friday evening.
   2 Claire _____ (go) to Nicole's
     party on Wednesday evening.
   3 Claire _____ (go) to the dentist
     on Thursday afternoon.
   4 Claire and Tom _____ (have)
     breakfast on Tuesday morning.
   5 Claire _____ (play) golf on
     Friday morning.
   6 Claire and her children _____
     (go) to the cinema on Monday evening.
   7 Claire and Jen _____ (have)
     a meeting on Thursday morning.

6 ★★★ **Write the questions for the answers about Claire's week. Use the present continuous.**

0 *Is Claire going to the dentist on Thursday?*

Yes, she is. Her appointment is at 4 pm.

1 _____

No, they're having breakfast.

2 _____

No, she's flying in the evening.

3 _____

Yes, but they don't know what film to see yet.

4 _____

That's right. They're playing in the afternoon.

7 ★★☆ **Mark the sentences P (present) or F (future arrangement).**

0 Henry's not at home. He's fishing with his dad. `P`

1 Sorry, I can't help you. I'm studying. ☐

2 Are you doing anything this evening? ☐

3 Look at the baby! She's trying to walk. ☐

4 Is Aunt Mary coming to stay next week? ☐

5 We're going to the skatepark this afternoon. ☐

6 I'm staying at my friend's house on Friday. ☐

8 ★★★ **Write five arrangements you have for this weekend. Use the present continuous.**

Adverbs

→ SB p.97

9 ★☆☆ **Read the sentences. Write the names under the pictures.**

Bella paints really well.

Molly paints quite badly.

Tom rides his bike dangerously.

Sam rides his bike carefully.

0 _____*Molly*_____ **2** _____

1 _____ **3** _____

10 ★★☆ **Unscramble the words to make adjectives. Then write the adverbs.**

		adjective	adverb
0	saye	*easy*	*easily*
1	wols		
2	kiquc		
3	souranged		
4	revosun		
5	teiqu		
6	dab		
7	larefuc		
8	dogo		

11 ★★★ Circle **the correct words.**

0 Jackson played very *good /(well)* and won the match *easy /(easily)*.

1 It was an *easy / easily* test and I finished it really *quick / quickly*.

2 My dad isn't a very *careful / carefully* driver and sometimes he drives quite *dangerous / dangerously*.

3 Please be *quiet / quietly* in the library – you can talk, but not too *loud / loudly*.

4 I didn't do *good / well* in the test – I had a really *bad / badly* day.

5 He's quite a *nervous / nervously* person and he talks really *quiet / quietly*.

GET IT RIGHT!

Adverbs

Adverbs usually come immediately after the object of the sentence or after the verb (if there is no object). They never come between the verb and the object.

✓ He drives his car dangerously.

✗ He ~~drives dangerously~~ his car.

Rewrite the sentences. Change the adjective in brackets into an adverb and put it in the correct place.

0 He can run fast, but he can't swim. (good)

He can run fast, but he can't swim well.

1 You should drive when it's raining. (slow)

_____

2 Hold the baby. (careful)

_____

3 We were walking because we were late for school. (fast)

_____

4 They did the homework because they worked together. (easy)

_____

VOCABULARY
Places in town

→ SB p.94

1 ★☆☆ **Look at the pictures and complete the words for places.**

0 c_o_nc_e_rt h_a_ll

4 p__l__ce st__t____n

1 b__s st__t ____n

5 p __ st __ff__ c__

2 f__ __ tb__ll st__d__ __ m

6 sp__rts c__ntr__

3 c__r p__r k

7 s__op __in__ m__ll

2 ★★☆ **Complete the text with words from Exercise 1.**

Our town is great. It's got everything I need. There's a really good sports ⁰_____centre_____ . You can do lots of different sports. There's a big ¹_____ hall as well, and I often go to see my favourite bands there. Most Saturdays, I go to the football ²_____ to see our football team play. There's a really big shopping ³_____ with lots of shops in it. And if you ever get bored, you can go to the bus ⁴_____ to catch a bus and visit another town.

3 ★★★ **Where are these people? Choose from the places in Exercise 1.**

0 'What time does the swimming pool close?'   _sports centre_

1 'I want to send this letter to Australia.'   _____

2 'I think Manchester United are going to win today.'   _____

3 'What time is the next bus to Liverpool?'   _____

4 'I want to buy some new shoes.'   _____

5 'The band starts playing at 8 pm.'   _____

6 'It costs £2 for every hour we stay.'   _____

7 'There's a problem at the bank. Come quickly.'   _____

Things in town: compound nouns

→ SB p.97

4 ★☆☆ **Write compound nouns using a word from each list.**

bill | ~~cycle~~ | graffiti | litter | speed | youth | zebra

bin | board | camera | club | crossing | ~~lane~~ | wall

0 _____cycle lane_____   4 _____

1 _____   5 _____

2 _____   6 _____

3 _____

5 ★★☆ **Match the nouns from Exercise 4 with the definitions.**

0 It checks how fast cars are going.   _speed camera_

1 You can ride your bike safely here.   _____

2 It advertises things on the side of the road.   _____

3 Cross the road safely here.   _____

4 A great place for young artists to paint.   _____

5 A place to meet friends and have fun.   _____

6 Throw your rubbish in this.   _____

6 ★★☆ **Which of these sentences are true about your town? Correct the ones that are false.**

1 Cars always stop at zebra crossings.

2 There are lots of things for young people to do. There are graffiti walls and really good youth clubs.

3 Speed cameras make the roads safer.

4 You can get everywhere on your bike using cycle lanes.

5 People always use the litter bins to throw away rubbish.

6 There are lots of billboards.

7 The high street is full of shoppers at the weekend.

REFERENCE

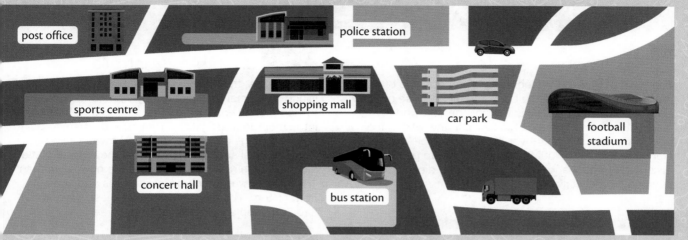

post office

police station

sports centre

shopping mall

car park

football stadium

concert hall

bus station

THINGS IN A TOWN

zebra crossing

youth club

speed camera

graffiti wall

cycle lane

litter bin

billboard

high street

VOCABULARY *EXTRA*

1 Match the words to make compound nouns.

0	play	a	way	0	_playground_
1	air	b	station	1	_____
2	motor	c	port	2	_____
3	city	d	ground	3	_____
4	under	e	centre	4	_____
5	railway	f	ground	5	_____

2 Write the name of a place in your country for each of these things.

1 A football stadium: _____

2 A city with an underground: _____

3 A busy motorway: _____

4 The nearest playground to your school: _____

5 An interesting city centre: _____

6 The biggest airport: _____

93

UNUSUAL TOWNS

 Monowi, US

The town of Monowi in Nebraska is perhaps one of the most unusual places in the US – and all because of Elsie Eiler. That's because Elsie is the only person who lives there. Monowi was never a big town. In the 1930s, the population was 150, but over the years people slowly started leaving. In 2000, there were only two people left: Elsie and her husband, Rudy. When Rudy died, Elsie became the only citizen.

 Thames Town, China

Shanghai is one of China's biggest cities. But just outside of Shanghai is a very different place called Thames Town. It cost £500 million to build and it is part of their 'One City, Nine Towns' project. When you walk down the streets there, you can easily forget you are in China!

That's because Thames Town is a copy of an English town. The streets and the buildings all look English. It has red phone boxes, London street signs, fish and chip shops and English pubs. There are also statues of Harry Potter and James Bond. Elsewhere in China, you can find the Eiffel Tower, an Austrian village and even Stonehenge.

 Sheffield, Australia

In the 1980s, the citizens of Sheffield on the Australian island of Tasmania decided they wanted more tourists to visit their town. They had an idea to turn their streets into an outdoor art gallery. They asked artists to paint huge paintings on the walls around town. Children from the local school helped, too – they painted little murals on the rubbish bins. There are now more than 100 murals, which include landscapes and scenes from history. The plan worked, and these days about 220,000 people visit Sheffield every year.

 Roswell, US

Some people believe that in 1947 an alien spacecraft crashed near the town of Roswell in New Mexico. They believe that the American military seized this UFO and took it to a secret place outside of the town. It's a strange idea, but people love mysteries like this. These days Roswell sees many tourists who are interested in life on other planets. There are lots of shops that sell souvenirs and there is one fast food restaurant with a UFO theme. There is also a museum about aliens.

1 _____

2 _____

📖 READING

1 **Read the article. Which towns can you see in the pictures? Write their names.**

2 **Read the article again. Write the names of the towns after the sentences.**

0 People think there were aliens here.   _Roswell_

1 They wanted more people to visit here. _____

2 It has a population of one. _____

3 It's near to a really big city. _____

4 People didn't want to live here. _____

5 It's like being in another country. _____

6 It's a mysterious place. _____

7 It's a great place if you like art. _____

3 **CRITICAL THINKING** **Fact or opinion? Mark the sentences F (fact) or O (opinion).**

1 The town of Monowi in Nebraska must be one of the most unusual places in the US. ☐

2 When Rudy died, Elsie became the only citizen. ☐

3 Thames Town cost £500 million to build. ☐

4 You can easily forget you are in China! ☐

5 Children from the local school helped, too. ☐

6 It's a strange idea, but people love mysteries like this. ☐

An informal email

 Jess
jessjones@thinkmail.com

Hi Jess,

Thanks for your message. So sorry to hear about your accident – I'm really glad you're feeling better now.

I've got some big news: we're moving house next month! We're going to live in Bristol and we're leaving on 25 July. The new house is quite big and I'm finally going to have my own bedroom! I can't wait! The rooms look a bit sad at the moment, but we're going to paint the walls and get some new furniture.

So I'm starting in a new school in September! I'm a bit nervous about that. But it's exciting, too. I really love Bristol – it's got great shops and cinemas, and there's a cool skatepark near our house.

You must come to visit SOON. I miss you loads! We're going to have a party on the second Sunday in August! Do you want to come? Let me know.

Send my love to your mum.

Love,

Lauren

1 **INPUT** **Read Lauren's email and answer the questions.**

0 Why is Lauren writing to Jess?
To tell her she is moving to Bristol.

1 When are her family leaving their old home?
_____

2 Why is the new house especially good for Lauren?
_____

3 What are they going to do to make the house look better?
_____

4 How does Lauren feel about going to a new school?
_____

5 What is going to happen in August?
_____

2 **ANALYSE** **Read the email again and find expressions that mean the same as 1–4.**

1 I'm very sad about (your bad news)
_____

2 I'm excited
_____

3 I really want you to (do something)
_____

4 Say hello to (someone) from me
_____

WRITING TIP: an informal email

- We write informal emails to friends, family and people we know well.
- Informal emails should be friendly and show personal interest in the other person.
- Use informal language, for example, short forms, direct questions, exclamation marks (!) and dashes (–).
- Organise the email into paragraphs:
  - First, greet your friend and comment on any news from him/her.
  - Then give your news.
  - Write the facts but also describe how you feel and give your opinions.

3 **PLAN** **Choose ONE of these situations. Complete the plan with short notes for the email you are going to write.**

- Your friend from the country is coming to your town for the first time and wants to know what it's like. Write and tell them.
- You're going on a school trip to a big city. Write to a friend to give them the news and tell them a bit about the city you're going to visit.
- It's the first day of your holiday. Write to your friend and tell them about the town where you are staying and your plans for the holiday.

Paragraph 1	
Paragraph 2	
Paragraph 3	

4 **PRODUCE** **Write your email to a friend in about 120–150 words.**

 **LISTENING**

1 🔊 **10.01** **Listen to the conversations and tick (✓) the correct box in the table.**

	Invitation accepted	Invitation not accepted
Conversation 1		
Conversation 2		
Conversation 3		

2 🔊 **10.01** **Listen again and complete the sentences.**

Conversation 1

Hannah invites Daniel to the ⁰ *sports centre* .

He can't go because he's got ¹_____ .

Daniel says they can go ²_____ .

Conversation 2

Isabelle invites Marcus to a ³_____ on
⁴_____ .

The ticket costs ⁵_____ .

They are going to meet outside the ⁶_____ at 8.

Conversation 3

Chloe says she hasn't got any ⁷_____ for
the ⁸_____ .

Luke and his friends are thinking of going to the
⁹_____ .

Chloe is interested in going to the ¹⁰_____
on Ice.

DIALOGUE

3 🔊 **10.02** **Complete the two conversations with the sentences A–H. Then listen and check.**

A How about next week?

B We're meeting outside the concert hall at 8.

C That would be great!

D I've got music practice this afternoon.

E See you then.

F Let's see.

G No! Sorry.

H How much is the ticket?

Conversation 1

Hannah Hi, Daniel. Do you want to go to the sports centre after school today?

Daniel Hannah, hi! No, sorry, I can't. ⁰*D*

Hannah What about tomorrow?

Daniel Yes, I think I can. ¹__ I'm meeting Martin.

Hannah Are you free any day this week?

Daniel No, I'm really busy. ²__

Hannah OK. ³__

Conversation 2

Isabelle Marcus, would you like to come to the Jax concert with us on Wednesday?

Marcus Wow! Yes, please. ⁴__ ! Thanks, Isabelle!

Isabelle We've got an extra ticket because Callum can't come.

Marcus Cool! ⁵__

Isabelle It's only £25 because it's a student ticket. ⁶__ Is that OK?

Marcus Great. ⁷__ .

4 **Write two short conversations for these situations.**

Conversation 1	**Conversation 2**
Boy invites girl to cinema.	Girl invites boy to party.
She says yes.	He asks what day and where.
They agree on a time.	He can't make it and says why.

Train to TH!NK

Problem solving

5 **The town council has money to build one new building. Look at the suggestions and match them with the advantages and disadvantages.**

> bad for shops on high street | creates lots of jobs
> ~~good to get bands into town~~ | more cars in town
> noisy at night | stops people parking on street

Suggestions	Advantage	Disadvantage
1 concert hall	*good to get bands into town*	
2 shopping mall		
3 car park		

6 **Think of an advantage and a disadvantage for these three suggestions.**

Suggestions	Advantage	Disadvantage
1 football stadium		
2 bus station		
3 sports centre		

7 **Complete the statement. Use your own ideas.**

I think the _____ is the best idea

because _____

and _____ .

> **PRONUNCIATION**
> Voiced /ð/ and unvoiced /θ/ consonants
> Go to page 121. 🎧

A2 Key for Schools

 READING AND WRITING
Part 5: open cloze

1 For each question, write the correct answer. Write ONE word for each gap.

✉ New message — ✎ ✕

A WEEKEND VISIT

I ⁰_____*am*_____ really excited! Next weekend, we are going to stay with my uncle and ¹_____ family. They live ²_____ a really nice flat near the city centre. My uncle is planning a busy weekend ³_____ us. We are going to walk around ⁴_____ city on Saturday morning. In the afternoon, my cousin Milly and I want to visit a museum ⁵_____ the rest of the family go on a boat on the river. On Sunday, we're all going to the stadium to ⁶_____ a rugby match. It's going to be the best weekend ever!

EXAM GUIDE: READING AND WRITING PART 5

In A2 Key for Schools Reading and Writing Part 5, you have to complete a short email or message. There is an example at the beginning and then you have to write ONE word in each of the six gaps.

- This exercise focuses on grammar, so you need to think about verbs, questions, negatives, prepositions, articles and pronouns.
- Always look at the words immediately <u>before</u> and <u>after</u> the gaps because they can help you find the right word.
- Try a word in the gap, then read the sentence again to see if it sounds right.

Contracted verb forms are not tested in this part of the exam.

2 For each question, write the correct answer. Write ONE word for each gap.

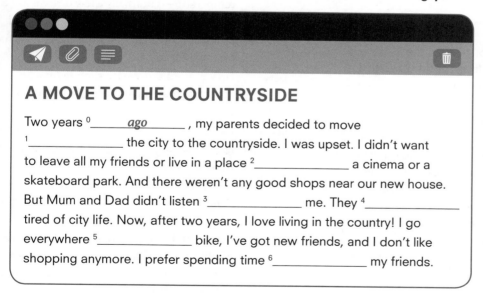

A MOVE TO THE COUNTRYSIDE

Two years ⁰_____*ago*_____ , my parents decided to move ¹_____ the city to the countryside. I was upset. I didn't want to leave all my friends or live in a place ²_____ a cinema or a skateboard park. And there weren't any good shops near our new house. But Mum and Dad didn't listen ³_____ me. They ⁴_____ tired of city life. Now, after two years, I love living in the country! I go everywhere ⁵_____ bike, I've got new friends, and I don't like shopping anymore. I prefer spending time ⁶_____ my friends.

CONSOLIDATION

🎧 LISTENING

1 🔊 **10.04** **Listen to the conversations. Choose the correct answer A, B or C. Then listen and check.**

1 What kind of holiday is Emma going to suggest to her parents?

  A hotel   **B** houseboat   **C** camping

2 Who's got the best idea about what they can do?

  A Mike   **B** Dad   **C** Mum

3 When are Emma and her family going on holiday?

  A 4 July   **B** 18 July   **C** 8 August

2 🔊 **10.04** **Listen again and answer the questions.**

0 Why don't Mike and Emma want to go to the same hotel as last year?

  They think it would be boring.

1 What does Emma think of the idea of a camping holiday?

  _____

2 What does Dad think about Emma's suggestion of a holiday on a houseboat?

  _____

3 What is Mum going to suggest to the grandparents?

  _____

4 Mum makes a joke. What does she say?

  _____

5 How soon are Emma and her family going on their holiday?

  _____

📖 VOCABULARY

3 **Circle the correct words.**

Before you go on a holiday, you need to think carefully about where you want to go. If you decide to go to a place in the ⁰(mountains)/ beach, for example, you have to know that the weather can be ¹*freezing / hot* (even in summer), and it can also be quite ²*windy / warm*. Everybody knows that deserts are ³*dry / wet*, but people sometimes forget that a ⁴*beach / forest* holiday means you are close to a lot of water, so the air can be quite ⁵*dry / humid*. This can mean you feel ⁶*hotter / colder* and not everybody likes that. Here are my family's plans for our next holiday. My parents love sailing, so we're going to ⁷*spend / spending* two weeks camping near a ⁸*hill / lake*. Then, on 1 September, we are ⁹*leaving / leave* for a weekend in the mountains.

4 **Complete the sentences. Use the words in the list.**

billboard | ~~concert hall~~ | cycle lane | litter bin
post office | speed camera | zebra crossing

0 I can't believe we can't get tickets for the show. There's room for 2,000 people in the <u>concert hall</u>.

1 I need some stamps. Can you go to the _____ for me?

2 Careful – don't drive so fast! There's a _____ ahead, so keep to 50 km/h, OK?

3 I want to throw this paper away. Is there a _____ around here?

4 Did you see that driver?! There was someone on the _____ and he didn't stop!

5 A road is much safer for cycling if there's a _____ .

6 There was an advertisement for his new album on the _____ .

⚙️ GRAMMAR

5 **Circle the correct words.**

Laurence When are you going on holiday?

Oscar Next weekend. And we're all looking forward to it. It's going to be the ⁰*better /*(best) holiday ever!

Laurence Are you going to the same place as last year?

Oscar Yes, we are. We had a brilliant time last year.

Laurence Is it ¹*hotter / hottest* than here?

Oscar Not really. It's ²*more cold / colder* than here, and there's usually ³*more / most* wind. So the temperature is normally a few degrees lower ⁴*more / than* here.

Laurence I think it's the ⁵*more / most* beautiful beach on the west coast.

Oscar Do you think so? Well, it's ⁶*more / most* attractive than other places, but we can't swim in the ocean.

Laurence Can't you?

Oscar No, the water is just too cold. And I don't think it's ⁷*safe / safely*.

Laurence Oh, really. Are there any ⁸*dangerous / dangerously* fish?

Oscar I don't think there are. But the waves are really high because of the wind. You have to be able to swim really ⁹*good / well* to go in the sea. But then you get out ¹⁰*quick / quickly* because it's freezing!

DIALOGUE

6 🔊 **10.05** **Complete the conversation. Use the phrases in the list.**

> are going to | busy with | can't
> can't go | going to come | ~~going to go~~
> I'd | like | like to | no problem

Eva Jack, I'm ⁰ ___*going to go*___ to the concert on Saturday. Would you ¹_____ to come along? My friend Nick ²_____ , so I've got a ticket if you want it.

Jack Saturday? I'm sorry, I can't. I'm ³_____ a project.

Eva I see. Well, maybe another time.

Jack Yeah, thanks for asking. Oh, would you and Nick ⁴_____ come over to our place next Sunday, maybe? We can sit in the garden and enjoy the beautiful weather. George and Camilla ⁵_____ come, too.

Eva ⁶_____ love to. That would be great. Let me talk to Nick. I know he's going to visit some relatives on Saturday, but I think he's ⁷_____ back on Sunday morning. So it should be fine. Can I tell you this evening?

Jack ⁸_____ . Talk to Nick first and call me any time.

Later, on the phone ...

Jack Hello?

Eva Oh, hi, Jack. It's about next Sunday. I'm really sorry. Nick ⁹_____ make it on Sunday. He's coming back late in the evening, so I'm going to come alone.

Jack OK.

📖 READING

7 **Read the magazine article about Peru. For questions 1–3, choose the correct ending (A or B) for each sentence.**

0 Peru is very popular for holidays ...
  Ⓐ because there are lots of beautiful places to visit.
  B because the weather is always sunny.

1 A holiday on the coast in summer is good if you ...
  A like hot, dry weather.
  B don't mind a lot of foggy and rainy days.

2 In the Andes, in winter it's usually ...
  A foggy but not very cold.
  B dry, and it can be very, very cold.

3 In the east, there are no mountains and ...
  A the weather doesn't change much.
  B there are extreme differences between seasons.

SO MANY KINDS OF WEATHER!

Peru isn't just a beautiful country. Tourists love it because of its attractive jungles, its stunning beaches and the fantastic Peruvian food. And many people come to see Machu Picchu, a very interesting Inca site that's more than 500 years old. But Peru is also famous for its many different climates. If you travel from one place to another, you can have very different weather on the same day! The weather on the coast is usually dry and warm, often hot. In the summer, it's hardly ever rainy there. In winter, the coast is often foggy, and the fog even has its own name, *garúa*. In the areas near the ocean, the so-called 'rainy season' starts around late May and comes to an end in October. In the mountains, the famous Andes, it's often cool, and sometimes cold. The summers there are usually rainy, but the winters are very dry, and can be freezing. In the east, where there are no mountains, the weather is usually hot and humid all year round.

✏️ WRITING

8 **Write a paragraph about the weather in your country (about 80–100 words). Think about these questions.**

- What's the weather like in your area? What's the weather like in different parts of the country?
- When are the best times of the year for tourists to visit your country?

11 FUTURE BODIES

Grammar rap!

▶32

Ⓖ GRAMMAR

will / won't for future predictions

→ SB p.104

1 ★★☆ **Put the words in order to make sentences.**

0 'll / home / by / I / 7.30 / be
I'll be home by 7.30.

1 Sunday / home / and / we / stay / at / relax / On / 'll
_____

2 homework / your / finish / Will / soon / you
_____

3 you / I / to / know / where / find / Will
_____

4 come / the / party / to / won't / Sebastian
_____

2 ★★☆ **Complete the sentences. Use *will* and the verb in brackets. Then match sentences 1–5 with sentences a–f.**

0 Don't worry. I'm sure you _____*won't have*_____ problems with the test. (not have) [e]

1 This year at school _____ cool. (be) ☐

2 I'm not sure a picnic is such a great idea. ☐

3 Kate's not sure if she _____ to the cinema tonight. (go) ☐

4 Brett and Mason _____ back from their trip soon. (be) ☐

5 Don't try to repair your bike without me. ☐

a Our teachers _____ probably _____ us to a youth camp in the last week before the holidays. (take)

b Perhaps she _____ at home and work on her project. (stay)

c It _____ probably _____ raining later today. (start)

d I'm sure they _____ lots of stories to tell. (have)

e You always study hard.

f Let's do it together. That _____ much more fun. (be)

3 ★★☆ **Complete the questions. Use *will* and the verbs in the list.**

get married | go | have (x 2) | ~~learn~~ | live

0 When _____*will*_____ you _____*learn*_____ to drive?

1 _____ you ever _____ in another country?

2 _____ you ever _____ a sports car?

3 How many children _____ you _____ ?

4 Do you think you _____ ?

5 _____ you _____ to university after school?

4 ★★★ **Complete the answers. Use *will* and the verbs in the list. Then match them with the questions in Exercise 3.**

do | drive | ~~have~~ | live | not get | take

0 I _____*'ll have*_____ lots. I love children. [3]

1 Yes, I think I _____ that but I'm not sure what to study yet. ☐

2 Yes, I think so. But actually, I'm sure I _____ married before I'm 30. ☐

3 I think I _____ my driving test before I go to university. ☐

4 A sports car? No. I don't think I _____ ever even _____ a car. ☐

5 I think I _____ in Japan for a year before I go to university. ☐

5 ★★★ **Answer the questions in Exercise 3 so they are true for you.**

_____
_____
_____
_____
_____
_____

PRONUNCIATION
The /h/ consonant sound Go to page 121. 🎧

First conditional

→ SB p.106

6 ★★☆ **Match each picture with two sentences.**

0 I won't have a lot of money left if I order an ice cream. **[b]**

1 If his alarm clock doesn't ring, he won't wake up. ☐

2 The neighbours will get angry if he doesn't stop. ☐

3 If I don't have a snack now, I'll be hungry later. ☐

4 He'll be late for school if he doesn't get up soon. ☐

5 If he doesn't practise, he'll never play in a band. ☐

7 ★★☆ **For each sentence, choose the most likely ending, A or B.**

0 He won't pass the test
 (A) if he doesn't study hard.
 B if he studies hard.

1 I'm sure all of your friends will come to your party
 A if you don't invite them.
 B if you invite them.

2 It's raining. If you don't put on your hat,
 A you'll get wet.
 B you won't get wet.

3 She'll book a trip to Rome
 A if it isn't too expensive.
 B if it's too expensive.

4 If we don't play better,
 A we'll win the match.
 B we'll lose the match.

5 If they find another of those T-shirts,
 A they won't get one for you.
 B they'll get one for you.

8 ★★★ **Complete the first conditional sentences with the correct form of the verbs.**

0 If you _don't listen_ (not listen), your teacher _won't tell_ (not tell) you what to do again.

1 If we _____ (not feed) the cat, she _____ (be) very hungry.

2 The police _____ (stop) him if he _____ (not slow down).

3 If we _____ (not use) a satnav, we _____ (not find) the way home.

4 Nobody _____ (talk) to them if they _____ (not be) friendly.

5 If Susie _____ (not help) me, I _____ (be) in trouble.

9 ★★★ **Complete the sentences with your predictions.**

50 years from now …

1 If all cars are driverless, _____.

2 If time travel becomes possible, _____.

3 If there are 10 billion people on Earth, _____.

4 If computers can speak all languages, _____.

5 If people can fly to Mars in 24 hours, _____.

Time clauses with *when* / *as soon as*

→ SB p.107

10 ★★☆ (Circle) **the correct words.**

0 When we (arrive)/ *'ll arrive*, we *send* / ('ll send) you a text message.

1 He *look* / *'ll look* for the keys as soon as he *'s* / *'ll be* home.

2 We *watch* / *'ll watch* the film as soon as the electricity *comes* / *will come* back on.

3 As soon as I *get* / *'ll get* the money, I *pay* / *'ll pay* you back.

4 I *take* / *'ll take* you to the new club when you *come* / *'ll come* and see us.

5 Dad *returns* / *will return* from the US as soon as his job there *is* / *will be* finished.

GET IT RIGHT!

First conditional

We use the present simple in the *if clause* and *will* / *won't* in the <u>result</u> clause. We never use *will* / *won't* in the *if clause*.

✓ *If I see Rory, I'll tell him the news.*

✗ *If I will see Rory, I'll tell him the news.*

Find four incorrect uses of *will*. Correct them.

I don't know what to do! I feel ill, but if I won't go to school tomorrow, I'll miss the test. If I'll miss the test, I'll have to do it in the holidays. I won't be able to go to London if I will have to do the test in the holidays. But if I will go to school tomorrow and do the test when I'm ill, I'm sure I won't get a good mark. What a difficult decision!

VOCABULARY
Parts of the body

→ SB p.104

1 ★☆☆ Unscramble the words to make parts of the body.

> alenk | asmotch | bolwe
> elusmc | cnek | ilp | tatroh

0 ___ankle___ 4 _____

1 _____ 5 _____

2 _____ 6 _____

3 _____

2 ★★☆ Complete the sentences with words for parts of the body.

0 When he tried to put his shoe on his f_oot_ , he found that his a_nkle_ hurt.

1 This backpack is so heavy that all the m_____s in my n_____ and my s_____ s are hurting.

2 I've got a lot of pain all up my left arm. It hurts from the ends of my f_____ s, through my h_____ , and up to my e_____ .

3 I walked straight into a window. My whole face really hurts; my l_____ , my m_____ , my e_____s and my e_____s – they all hurt!

4 I ate too much. I've got s_____ ache.

3 ★★☆ Write verbs or phrases for actions that match the parts of the body. How many can you find?

foot – _run, walk,_ _____

mouth – _eat_ _____

ear – _listen to music,_ _____

arm – _____

eye – _____

fingers – _____

tongue – _____

when and *if*

→ SB p.107

4 ★☆☆ Circle the correct words.

0 Mum doesn't know when she'll be back. She'll phone us (if) / when she has to work late.

1 I can't do that now. I'll try to do it tomorrow *if* / *when* I've got time.

2 I'm not sure where my tablet is right now. I'll give it to you *if* / *when* I find it.

3 It's still dark outside. We'll start in an hour, *if* / *when* it's light.

4 It's Jane's birthday on Sunday. She'll be sad *if* / *when* you don't give her a present.

5 I'm checking my messages now. I'll be with you in a minute *if* / *when* I finish.

WordWise:
Expressions with *do*

→ SB p.105

5 ★☆☆ Match the sentences with the pictures.

0 Let's go in there. They do great food. `c`

1 I'm happy to do the cooking, but it seems we need to go shopping first. ☐

2 I think we need to do some cleaning here. ☐

3 This has the latest technology. It does 30 kilometres to the litre. ☐

4 And Dad thinks I'm doing my homework. Ha ha ha! ☐

5 He isn't very well at the moment. I don't think he can play in the match today. ☐

6 ★★☆ Complete the questions with the words in the list.

> cooking | ~~exercise~~ | homework | ice cream | well

0 A How often do you do _exercise_ in a week?
  B I go running on Mondays and Wednesdays, and go to the gym on Fridays.

1 A Did you do _____ in your last English test?
  B Yes, I got top marks.

2 A Who does the _____ in your family?
  B My mum. Her food is really good.

3 A Who does the best _____ in your town?
  B There's a new café on my street. It's wonderful.

4 A When do you usually do your _____ ?
  B Straight after school, when I can still remember everything.

7 ★★★ Answer the questions in Exercise 6 so they are true for you.

REFERENCE

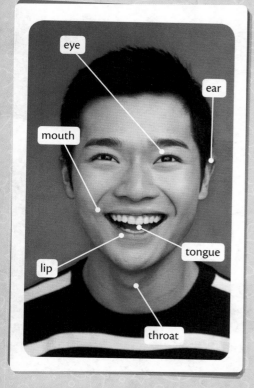

eye
ear
mouth
lip
tongue
throat

PARTS OF THE BODY

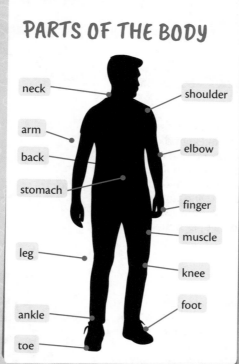

neck
arm
back
stomach
leg
ankle
toe
shoulder
elbow
finger
muscle
knee
foot

ACHES

stomach ache

ear ache

headache

toothache

WHEN / IF

When we arrive, John will cook the dinner. (It is certain we will arrive.)

If we arrive before 10, John will cook the dinner. (It isn't certain we will arrive before 10.)

EXPRESSIONS WITH *DO*

do exercise
do the cleaning
do the cooking

do homework
do OK
do well

do (food / drink, in a café, restaurant, etc.)
do (12 kilometres to the litre)

VOCABULARY *EXTRA*

1 **Unscramble the letters and write the words under the pictures.**

eckhe | eehtt | dahe | irha | kins | reath

0 ___*cheek*___   1 _____   2 _____   3 _____   4 _____   5 _____

2 **Complete the sentences with the words in Exercise 1. Make them plural if you need to.**

0 You should brush your ____*teeth*____ after every meal.
1 Penny has got lovely long brown _____ .
2 I was scared and my _____ was beating very fast.
3 My _____ is really dry. I need some cream.
4 Is it cold outside? Your nose and _____ are red!
5 Matt's very tall. The top of my _____ only reaches his shoulder!

FROM SCIENCE FICTION TO SCIENCE FACT

Technology is moving fast and changing our lives. We asked YOU, our readers, to tell us about inventions that you think will change our world and our health in the future!

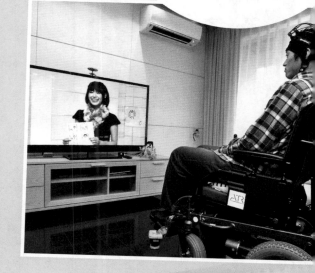

1 _____

Hospitals already have some amazing machines, but soon they'll have robot nurses, too! Just like Baymax in *Big Hero 6*! I don't think people will wake up and find a robot standing next to their bed any time soon, but I read that scientists in Japan are creating robots to do some of the jobs nurses do. Robots will be useful for lifting and moving patients. This sounds great because if robots do the heavy work, nurses will have more time to look after individual patients.

Anton

2 _____

If you cut your leg or finger, it usually gets better quickly. But lots of people have very bad injuries that don't heal easily. The other day, I watched a video about a new gel to help these people. It seems to have incredible healing effects and I'm sure doctors will use it in the future. It made me think of a *Star Wars* film, when Luke Skywalker floated in a bath of healing gel to repair his body. Maybe that's where scientists got this idea!

Lachlan

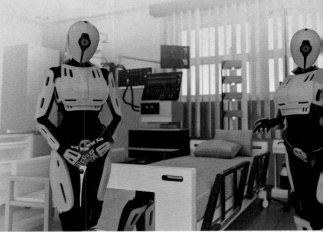

3 _____

Yesterday, I read a great article about mind control. Scientists are now making a wheelchair you can control with your mind. When you think about where you want to go, the chair moves in the right direction. It means that users will be more independent. At the moment, the wheelchair can follow simple instructions like: *stop* or *go right*. It also has technology to stop it from hitting walls and furniture. Scientists are still working on it, so when it's ready, it will probably be able to do more.

Phoebe

📖 READING

1 Read the blog. Match the headings with the paragraphs.

A Just think and move

B Computers that care for you

C A magical medicine

2 Match the comments with the paragraphs.

A I can't move my arms and legs. This will change my life. I hope I'll have one soon. ☐

B Great idea. It will help people get better more quickly. ☐

C I don't like this idea. When I'm really ill I want real people to help me! Old people and children won't like these, I'm sure. ☐

3 CRITICAL THINKING Complete the table with your ideas.

Invention	Who will this help?	Disadvantages
Robot nurses		
Healing gel		
Mind-controlled wheelchair		

DEVELOPING ⟩ *Writing*

Taking phone messages

1 **INPUT** **🔊 11.02** **Listen to the conversation. Why can't Dylan take the call? Choose the correct answer.**

A He's out at the bank.
B He's out shopping.
C He's in a meeting.

2 **🔊 11.02** **Listen again. Then read Rachel's message for Dylan. Which two pieces of information in the message are wrong?**

1 _____
2 _____

> Dylan
> Gavin called from the fruit and vegetable company. He says he had a problem with his van and he's going to be late. He'll arrive at 5 pm. He doesn't have any tomatoes, but he asked if you want anything else instead. You can call him on his mobile.
> I'm going home now, but I'll see you next Saturday.
> Rachel

3 **ANALYSE** **Later, Rachel wrote this message to her mum. Compare it with her first message. Complete the sentences with the correct name, Dylan or Mum.**

> Mum
> Back from café. Julia phoned. Said yoga class is at 6 tomorrow. Asked if you need lift – can pick you up at 5.30. Will ring again later.
> Going to Fran's now. Back about 7 – see you then.
> Love,
> Rach

1 The message to _____ is informal.
2 The message to _____ is quite formal.
3 In the message to _____ Rachel wrote in full sentences.
4 In the message to _____ she left out some words.

4 **Rewrite Rachel's message to her mum in full sentences. Use the missing words in the list. You can use some words more than once.**

> a | at | I | I'll | I'll be | I'm | she | the

I'm back from the café.

✏️ WRITING TIP: taking a phone message

Listen carefully and make notes about the most important details:
- Who phoned?
- Who is the message for?
- What is the key information?

After the phone call, write out the message. If it's for someone you know well, you can leave out some words – but only if the message is still clear:
- articles (*the, a, an*)
- personal pronouns (*I, we, he, she*)
- possessive adjectives (*my, his, their*)
- verb *to be* (*am, is, are*)

5 **Make this message more informal. Cross out the words that can be left out.**

> Noah
> Thomas called. He wants to ask you about the French homework. He's finding it hard to understand. Also he's going to see the new film at the cinema tonight. Are you interested? Can you please contact him as soon as possible? His new phone number is 0679 645036.
> Robbie

6 **🔊 11.03** **PLAN** **Listen to the conversations and make notes.**

Call from: _____
Message for: _____
Information: _____
_____
_____

Call from: _____
Message for: _____
Information: _____
_____
_____
_____

7 **PRODUCE** **Write your two phone messages.**
- Decide whether the message is formal or informal.
- Include all the important information.
- When your messages are finished, read them again. Ask yourself, 'Will the message be clear to the person who reads it?'

LISTENING

1 🔊 **11.04** Listen to the conversations. Choose the correct answer A, B or C.

Conversation 1

1 How does Lee feel about the Biology project?

　A fed up

　B excited

　C bored

Conversation 2

2 How does Ryan see the future of food?

　A We'll eat pills.

　B We won't eat cakes.

　C We'll still eat the same food.

Conversation 3

3 What does Milly think Sofia should do to get fit?

　A go to the gym

　B go dancing

　C walk on the beach

2 🔊 **11.04** Listen again and mark the sentences T (true) or F (false).

Conversation 1

1 Lee won't enjoy the project. ☐

2 Laura and Lee will have to work hard. ☐

Conversation 2

3 Ryan enjoys making cakes. ☐

4 Ava thinks that perhaps people will eat space food. ☐

Conversation 3

5 Milly is on her way to the park. ☐

6 Sofia likes going to the beach. ☐

DIALOGUE

3 🔊 **11.05** Complete the conversation with the words in the list. Then listen and check.

> poor | sorry to hear | what a shame

Alex Hi, Naomi. What seems to be the problem?

Naomi It's about Chris, my brother.

Alex What about him?

Naomi He's in hospital.

Alex I'm ¹_____ that, Naomi. What happened?

Naomi He broke his leg.

Alex ²_____ Chris!

Naomi Yes. We wanted to go to the concert on Sunday. Now we can't go.

Alex ³_____ .

4 Read the situation and complete the short conversation. Use phrases from Exercise 3 to express sympathy.

> Melissa notices that her friend Owen has a problem. She asks him about it and finds out that Owen lost his wallet on the way to the shopping centre. He lost all his money. He wanted to buy a new games controller and can't buy one now.

Melissa What seems to be the problem, Owen? You don't look very happy.

Owen _____

　　　 _____

　　　 _____

　　　 _____

　　　 _____

PHRASES FOR FLUENCY

5 🔊 **11.06** Read the two conversations. Replace the phrases in *italics* with the phrases in the list. Then listen and check.

> I can't wait. | I mean | I̶ ̶s̶u̶p̶p̶o̶s̶e̶ ̶s̶o̶.̶
> Tell you what. | Wait and see. | Whatever.

Conversation 1

Andy Looks like it'll start raining pretty soon.

Lexi ⁰*I think perhaps you're right.*

Andy ¹*I really don't care.* I've got so much work to do, so I can't go out anyway.

Lexi ²*Here's what I think.* I could help you, and then we could go out together. ³*What I want to say is*, if that's OK with you, of course.

Conversation 2

Grady ⁴*I'm very excited.* If the weather's OK on Saturday, we're going to go climbing. The mountain we want to climb is 3,560 metres high!

Anne Wow. That's a long way to climb! Do you think you'll get to the top?

Grady ⁵*We'll find out soon!*

0 _____*I suppose so.*_____

1 _____

2 _____

3 _____

4 _____

5 _____

A2 Key for Schools

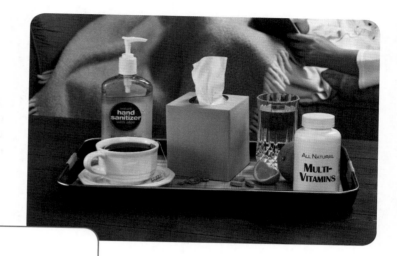

READING AND WRITING
Part 6: a short message

1 **Your friend, Morgan, is ill and didn't go to school this week. You want to go and see your friend.**

Write a message to Morgan. In your message:
- say you are sorry that Morgan is ill
- offer to visit
- ask how you can help

Write 25 words or more.

EXAM GUIDE: READING AND WRITING PART 6

In A2 Key for Schools Reading and Writing Part 6, you have to write a short message using at least 25 words.

There is a sentence to explain the situation and three items of information you must include in your message.

- Read the information about the situation very carefully.
- Read the three points you must include in the message. Make sure you write about all three points, not just one or two.
- Before you start writing, think about what you are going to say.
- What verb tenses do you need to use? Past, present or future?
- Make sure you start and finish your message correctly.
- The message is to a friend, so use friendly, informal language.
- You must write a minimum of 25 words, but you can write more, if you have time.

2 **Your friend Sam wants to start running every day. You want to join your friend. Write a message to Sam. In your message:**

- ask if you can go running with Sam
- recommend a good place to go running
- suggest a time to meet

Write 25 words or more.

12 TRAVEL THE WORLD

Grammar rap!

▶35

@ GRAMMAR
Present perfect simple
→ SB p.112

1 ★☆☆ **Find eleven more past participles in the puzzle. Use the irregular verb list on page 128 to help you.**

R	D	S	L	E	P	T	S	F
T	O	W	S	L	E	E	P	L
A	N	U	V	U	M	S	O	E
K	E	M	S	E	E	N	K	W
E	B	W	R	I	T	T	E	N
N	O	W	R	O	T	E	N	A
A	U	F	L	O	W	N	G	R
S	G	W	A	N	O	R	O	N
T	H	D	G	O	N	E	E	O
O	T	H	E	R	T	A	S	D

0	buy	*bought*		6	sleep	_____
1	do	_____		7	speak	_____
2	fly	_____		8	swim	_____
3	go	_____		9	take	_____
4	meet	_____		10	win	_____
5	see	_____		11	write	_____

2 ★★☆ **Complete the sentences with the past participles in Exercise 1.**

0 I have never ____*flown*____ in a plane.

1 My brother has _____ to a football match.

2 You don't want to watch that film – you've _____ it hundreds of times!

3 I'm having a great holiday. I've _____ hundreds of photographs!

4 She's really tired because she's _____ fifty emails today.

5 They haven't got any money left because they've _____ so many things.

6 We're really happy because we've _____ a competition.

7 The teacher's angry with us because we haven't _____ our homework.

3 ★★☆ **When Jenny was 12, she wrote a list of things she wanted to do. Jenny is now 75. Write sentences about what she has and hasn't done. Use the present perfect of the verbs.**

0 write a book ✓

1 see the Himalaya mountains ✓

2 fly in a hot air balloon ✗

3 meet the president ✗

4 sleep under the stars ✓

5 swim to France ✗

6 win a tennis tournament ✗

7 walk over the Golden Gate Bridge! ✓

0 *She's written a book.* _____

1 _____

2 _____

3 _____

4 _____

5 _____

6 _____

7 _____

been to vs. *gone to*
→ SB p.112

4 ★★☆ **Match the pictures with the sentences.**

In Beijing. Call me. Love, Jim

0 He's been to China.   `b`

1 He's gone to China.   ☐

2 They've been to the supermarket. ☐

3 They've gone to the supermarket. ☐

Present perfect with
ever / never
 → SB p.113

5 ★★☆ **Put the words in order to make questions and answers.**

0 **A** you / ever / a / won / Have / competition
Have you ever won a competition?

  B never / I've / No, / anything / won
No, I've never won anything.

1 **A** been / Has / New York / to / ever / she
_____

  B never / the US / she's / to / been / No,
_____

2 **A** you / eaten / ever / Have / food / Japanese
_____

  B restaurant / been / never / No, / a Japanese / I've / to
_____

3 **A** ever / they / a helicopter / Have / flown / in
_____

  B never / in / flown / they've / a helicopter or a plane / No,
_____

4 **A** your parents / Have / ever / angry with you / been
_____

  B they've / angry / with me / lots of times / Yes, / been
_____

Present perfect vs. past simple → SB p.115

6 ★★☆ **Complete the conversations. Use the present perfect or past simple of the verbs.**

1 **A** Let's go to an Indian restaurant.
  B But I⁰ _____'ve never eaten_____ (never/eat) Indian food before.
  A No, you're wrong! You ¹_____ (eat) Indian food at my house last week.
  B Really? Oh yes – you ²_____ (make) a curry! I remember now.

2 **A** My parents ³_____ (travel) to lots of places round the world.
  B ⁴_____ (they/visit) China?
  A Oh, yes, they ⁵_____ (go) to Beijing two years ago. They ⁶_____ (love) it there.
  B They're lucky. I ⁷_____ (always/want) to go to China, but I ⁸_____ (never/have) the chance.

PRONUNCIATION
Sentence stress **Go to page 121.**

7 ★★★ **Complete the email. Use the present perfect or past simple of the verbs.**

> **Mark**
> markernest@thinkmail.com
>
> Hi Mark,
> It's August already! Sorry I ⁰ _____haven't written_____ (not write) to you recently – the thing is, I ¹_____ (be) really busy in June and July!
> Anyway, I've got news for you. Two important things ²_____ (happen) to me.
> So, my first big news is that last week I ³_____ (go) to a party at my friend's house and I ⁴_____ (meet) a really nice girl called Joanna.
> We ⁵_____ (talk) the whole evening and we ⁶_____ (get) on together really well.
> So that's good, eh? Only there's a problem, because at the end of the evening she ⁷_____ (ask) me to go ice skating with her. Of course I ⁸_____ (say) yes! But I ⁹_____ (never / try) ice skating before. Should I go? I don't want to look stupid, you know!
> The other news is that my parents ¹⁰_____ (find) a new flat. So next month we're moving to a different part of town. ¹¹_____ (you / hear) of Milson Road? That's where we're going. Mum's really pleased because the flat's got a garden, and that's one thing she ¹²_____ (always / want). But I'll be a bit sad to leave this place because I ¹³_____ (live) here all my life.
> Anyway, that's it for now. Write soon.
> Andy

GET IT RIGHT!
Present perfect with
ever / never

We use *never* when we want to say 'at no time in (my/your/his, etc.) life' and we use *ever* when we want to say 'at any time in (my/your/his, etc.) life'.

✓ *I've seen 'Black Panther'. It's the best film I've **ever** seen.*

✗ *I've seen 'Black Panther'. It's the best film I've ~~never~~ seen.*

Remember we don't use *not* and *never* together.

Circle the correct words.

0 Lindsay is the best friend I've *never* / (*ever*) had.

1 I've *never* / *ever* been to London, but I hope to go there next year.

2 I'm nervous about flying because I've *never* / *ever* been on a plane before.

3 I'm wearing my new shoes. They're the best shoes I've *never* / *ever* had.

4 I have *never* / *ever* visited Paris.

VOCABULARY
Transport and travel

→ SB p.115

1 ★☆☆ **Look at the pictures and complete the puzzle. What is the 'mystery' word?**

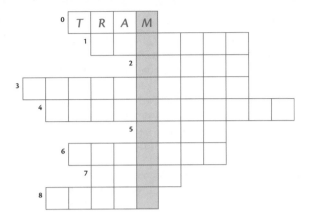

0	T	R	A	M

The mystery word is _____ .

2 ★★☆ **Match the forms of transport (1–8) with the definitions (a–i).**

0 a minibus — g
1 an underground train — ☐
2 a tram — ☐
3 a boat — ☐
4 a plane — ☐
5 a bicycle — ☐
6 a train — ☐
7 a scooter — ☐
8 a helicopter — ☐

a It's like a bus but it goes on tracks.
b It's got two wheels and a small motor.
c It travels on tracks and stops at stations.
d It flies but it's smaller than a plane.
e A train that travels below the city.
f It travels on the sea, lakes and rivers.
g A small bus for about ten people.
h It's got two wheels but no motor.
i It flies and carries hundreds of people.

Travel verbs

→ SB p.115

3 ★☆☆ **Complete the sentences with the verbs in the list.**

> catch | drive | flies | misses | ride | take

0 Aziz is a pilot. He ___flies___ A380 planes for Emirates Airlines.
1 I don't travel by car. I always _____ the train.
2 He hasn't got a car because he can't _____ .
3 She is always at the station ten minutes before her train leaves. She never _____ it.
4 Every weekend they _____ their motorbikes all the way to Scotland.
5 Please don't be late! We must _____ the 10.30 train.

4 ★★☆ **Complete the sentences. Use the correct form of the travel verbs in Exercise 3.**

0 Last year we _flew_ from London to Los Angeles.
1 Sometimes I'm late for school because I _____ the bus.
2 My mum _____ me to school every day – in her twenty-year-old car!
3 We never _____ our bikes when it rains. We catch the bus.
4 Are you going to _____ the 10 o'clock train?
5 When they got back to the airport, they _____ a taxi home.

REFERENCE

Travel verbs and transport

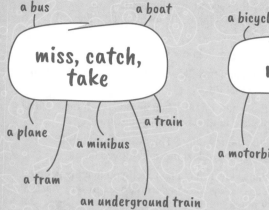

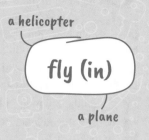

a bus   a boat

miss, catch, take

a plane   a minibus   a train

a tram

an underground train

a bicycle

ride

a scooter

a motorbike

a car

drive

a minibus

a helicopter

fly (in)

a plane

 VOCABULARY *EXTRA*

1 Circle the correct words.

0 He got *in* / *on* the train in London.
1 It was raining when she got *in* / *off* the taxi.
2 You have to get *off* / *out* of the bus at the next stop.

3 We got *on* / *off* the plane and looked for our seats.
4 Are you getting *on* / *in* this train?
5 He got *on* / *in* his bike and rode to the shop.

2 Write sentences to describe the pictures.

1 He's _____
2 She's _____
3 They're _____
4 They're _____

The two travellers

One evening, an old man was sitting on a bench on the top of a hill. He was looking down at the town where he lived in the valley below him.

Just then, a traveller walked up to him – a man carrying a stick with a small bag on it containing his possessions. He stopped beside the old man to talk to him.

'Excuse me, sir,' the traveller said. 'I am going to the town down there, the town in the valley. Do you know it?'

'Yes,' said the old man. 'I know it.'

'Well,' said the traveller. 'Can you tell me – what are the people like in that town?'

The old man thought for a bit. Then he said, 'Tell me – what were the people like in the last town you were in?'

'Oh,' said the traveller. 'They were awful – horrible people. They didn't like me, and I didn't like them.'

And the old man said, 'I'm sorry to tell you that the people in the town in the valley are horrible, too. You won't like them.'

'OK,' said the traveller. And he walked away. He didn't go to the town in the valley.

About an hour later, another traveller arrived near the old man.

'Excuse me, sir,' the second traveller said. 'I am going to the town down there, the town in the valley. Do you know it?'

'Yes,' said the old man. 'I know it.'

'Well,' said the second traveller. 'Can you tell me – what are the people like in that town?'

The old man thought for a bit. Then he said, 'Tell me – what were the people like in the last town you were in?'

'Oh,' said the second traveller. 'They were wonderful – really nice people. They liked me, and I loved them.'

And the old man said, 'I'm happy to tell you that the people in the town in the valley are wonderful, too. I'm sure you'll like them very much.'

'Oh, thank you!' said the second traveller. And he walked happily down to the town in the valley.

READING

1   Read the story and answer the questions.

   1   What question do the two travellers ask the old man?

     _____

   2   Which two words does the old man use to describe the people in his town?

     _____

2   Read the story again and answer the questions.

   0   What was the old man looking at when he was on the bench?

     He was looking at the town where he lived.

   1   What did the first traveller say about the people in the last town he visited?

     _____

   2   What did the first traveller decide to do after the old man's reply?

     _____

   3   What did the second traveller say about the people in the last town he visited?

     _____

   4   Where did the second traveller go when he left the old man?

     _____

3   **CRITICAL THINKING**   What does the story tell us? Choose A, B or C.

   A   When we travel to different places, we will meet all kinds of different people.

   B   Being warm and friendly changes the experiences we have with people.

   C   Before we visit a place, it's a good idea to ask questions about the people who live there.

4   **What do you think people should do when they visit new countries? Number the activities in order of importance for you.**

   ☐ Find out about the culture before going

   ☐ Go to local events

   ☐ Learn some phrases in the local language

   ☐ Speak to local people

   ☐ Meet other travellers

   ☐ Try the local food

   ☐ Visit famous tourist attractions

An essay

1 **INPUT** **Read the advertisement for a competition in a magazine and complete the notes.**

1 The competition is for young _____ .
2 The general topic of the essay is _____ .
3 The prize is _____ .

CALLING ALL YOUNG
TRAVEL WRITERS!

We want to hear about your travel experiences and plans – and YOU could win a prize!

Send us an essay about your travels:

- some places you have been to
- the best trip you have made – when and where did you go, and what did you do?
- a place you want to visit – why?

We'll publish the top three essays on our website and the winner will receive a digital camera!

2 **Read Rebecca's essay for the competition. Underline the information that the advertisement asks for in the essay.**

1 I haven't travelled a lot outside my country, but I've had some great holidays with my family. We've driven through the amazing countryside in the north, and we've gone skiing a few times in the mountains.

2 But the best trip I've ever had was when we travelled to the south of France last summer.
We flew to Paris, and the next day we caught the train to Avignon – the fastest train I've ever been on! During our week in Avignon, we explored the old city and took buses to some of the villages up in the hills. Also our hotel organised a minibus to take us to the coast. It was beautiful there, so I was sad when we had to leave.

3 Now I can't wait to go travelling again. My dream is to go to China because it looks so exciting and so different from my country.

3 **ANALYSE** **Read the essay again and complete the sentences with the number of the paragraph.**

0 Paragraph _3_ is about Rebecca's hopes for the future.
1 Paragraph __ introduces the topic of travelling.
2 Paragraph __ describes a particular set of events in the past.
3 Paragraph __ is about some of the travel experiences Rebecca has had in her life.
4 Paragraph __ explains why she wants to travel to a certain place.
5 Paragraph __ contains the most information.

WRITING TIP: an essay

- Use quite formal language in an essay.
- Organise the essay into paragraphs:
  - Start with a short introduction to the topic.
  - Give more detailed information in the main part of the essay.
  - Finish with a short conclusion or an explanation for something.
- Before you start writing, make a plan.

4 **PLAN** **Read the competition advert again and plan your essay. Think about the different tenses you need to use in the three parts of the essay.**

Paragraph 1	
Paragraph 2	
Paragraph 3	

5 **PRODUCE** **Now, use your notes in Exercise 4 to write your essay in 120–150 words.**

🎧 LISTENING

1 🔊 **12.02** **Listen to part of a radio phone-in programme and choose the correct words.**

1 Ross Edgley is *sailing / swimming* round the coast of Britain.

2 At the moment, he's in *Scotland / England*.

3 He's doing the trip *on his own / with a team*.

4 So far, the weather has *sometimes / never* been bad.

2 🔊 **12.02** **Listen again and ⟨circle⟩ Choose the correct answer A, B or C.**

0 How did Jacob find out about this story?

  A He met Ross Edgley.

  B He saw a video about it.

  Ⓒ He heard it on the news.

1 Where is Ross now?

  A Near the end of his journey

  B In the middle of his journey

  C 200 kilometres from the start of his journey

2 How far does he swim every day?

  A About 30 kilometres

  B About 6 kilometres

  C About 150 kilometres

3 During the trip, Ross hasn't

  A slept on the boat.

  B eaten much food.

  C walked on land.

4 Ross has had a problem with

  A his tongue.

  B his team.

  C his toe.

DIALOGUE

3 🔊 **12.03** **Match Jacob's answers with Tina's questions. There are two extra questions. Then listen and check.**

a Does he swim every day?

b How far has he swum?

c Does he have to eat special food?

d Do you know anything else about the trip?

e Has he had any problems so far?

f How long will the swim take?

g Has he seen any sharks?

h How far does he have to swim every day?

1 **Jacob**	About 150 days. He started in June and he should finish in November.	☐
2 **Jacob**	About 30 kilometres.	☐
3 **Jacob**	Well, I know that he isn't alone. He's got a team of people to help him.	☐
4 **Jacob**	Yes. He swims for six hours, then he returns to the boat for six hours to eat and sleep.	☐
5 **Jacob**	No, he doesn't, but he has to eat a lot of food because he gets hungry.	☐
6 **Jacob**	Well, there's been some bad weather, like very strong winds and storms.	☐

Train to TH!NK

Exploring differences

4 **Look at the table. Are the sentences true about only waiters, only taxi drivers, or both? Tick (✓) the correct column.**

You ...	waiters	taxi drivers	both
meet a lot of people.			✓
spend a long time on your feet.			
have to carry things.			
can work in any weather.			
have to remember things.			
wear special clothes.			

5 **Think about houses and flats. What things are the same? What things are different? Write three more things in the left-hand column. Tick (✓) the correct column.**

It ...	house	flat	both
has got bedrooms.			✓

A2 Key for Schools

READING AND WRITING
Part 3: 3-option multiple choice

1 **For these questions, choose the correct answer.**

> **This week we're interviewing Leila Moreton, a travel journalist. She tells us about her job ...**
>
> I've got the best job ever. I'm a journalist and I write about activity holidays for teenagers. I travel to new places to experience different holidays. Then, I write articles for travel magazines and websites.
>
> **Tell us about some of your experiences, Leila.**
>
> I've been sailing in Greece and I've been kayaking in Canada – not on holiday, but as research for my job! It isn't only about adventure – I've also learnt to make a video, how to cook and do circus skills! There are holidays for every interest.
>
> **How did you find your dream job?**
>
> Well, I've always loved writing. English was my best subject at school and I wrote for our school website. I also love travelling. When I was a child, we lived in South Africa for a few years because of my parents' jobs. It was a great opportunity to explore new places. When I finished school, I worked for a travel company and that's when I got interested in teen activity holidays. My job is perfect because I do my two favourite things: writing and travelling. I don't need holidays! In fact, I usually stay at home for my holidays because travel is work for me.
>
> **Have you enjoyed everything you've done?**
>
> Not everything! My job's fun, but I've discovered that I don't like riding horses or camels, and I'm frightened of flying in small planes and helicopters!

1 What does Leila do?
  A She's a travel agent.
  B She's a school teacher.
  C She's a travel writer.

2 Leila's interested in
  A exciting holidays.
  B learning new sports.
  C learning skills for work.

3 When Leila was a child, she
  A never went on holiday.
  B lived in a different country.
  C didn't speak English.

4 In her holidays, she
  A visits new places.
  B doesn't go away.
  C goes horse-riding.

5 Leila says she has
  A always had lots of fun.
  B never liked flying in planes.
  C learnt two things about herself.

EXAM GUIDE: READING AND WRITING PART 3

In A2 Key for Schools Reading and Writing Part 3, you have to read a short article and then answer five multiple-choice questions.

- First, read the article carefully. Don't worry about words you don't understand. Focus on the general meaning.
- Look at the first question and find the part of the text that it refers to.
- Read all the options carefully.
- Re-read the part of the text and choose the correct answer.
- You won't see the same words in the questions and the article, so look out for words and expressions that have the same meaning.
- The questions are always in the same order as the text.

CONSOLIDATION

🎧 LISTENING

1 🔊 **12.04** **Listen to the conversation. Choose the correct answer A, B or C.**

1 What happened to William?
  A He fell off his bike and hurt his shoulder.
  B He fell off his motorbike and hurt his back.
  C He fell off his motorbike and hurt his shoulder.

2 What does William think is dangerous?
  A driving in traffic
  B riding a bicycle
  C riding a motorbike

3 How does William usually get to work now?
  A by motorbike
  B by car
  C by bus

2 🔊 **12.04** **Listen again and answer the questions.**

0 When did William buy his motorbike?
  He bought it two weeks ago.

1 Why did he buy a motorbike?
  _____

2 Why doesn't he want to use the underground?
  _____

3 When will William get on his motorbike again?
  _____

4 What does he like about going to work by bus?
  _____

3 **Complete the sentences with *been* or *gone*.**

Tom Your dad travels a lot. Where is he this time?

Alice He's ⁰____*gone*____ to Brazil.

Tom Lucky him! Have you ever ¹_____ to Brazil?

Alice No, I haven't. I've never ²_____ anywhere outside Europe.

Tom Where's your sister by the way?

Alice She's ³_____ to the dentist's with my mum.

Tom I haven't ⁴_____ to the dentist's for a long time.

🅖 GRAMMAR

4 **Complete the conversations with the present perfect of the verbs.**

0 A Where's Martin?
  B I don't know. I *haven't seen* (not see) him today.

1 A Are Sam and Julia here?
  B No, they _____ (go) to the cinema.

2 A Is there any food in the kitchen?
  B No – my brother _____ (eat) it all!

3 A _____ (you / write) to your aunt?
  B Not yet. I'll do it tonight.

4 A Are you enjoying Los Angeles?
  B It's great. I _____ (meet) lots of nice people.

5 A Have you got a lot of homework?
  B No, only a little – and I _____ (do) it all!

6 A Is this a good book?
  B I don't know. I _____ (not read) it.

7 A Why are you so happy?
  B My parents _____ (give) me a new bike for my birthday!

🅰🅩 VOCABULARY

5 **Complete the words.**

0 Can we watch this film? I haven't s *e* *e* *n* it before, but everyone says it's great.

1 Some really rich people fly between cities by h_ _ _ _ _ _ _ _ _ .

2 He can't walk now because he's broken his a_ _ _ _ .

3 In some European cities you can still see t_ _ _s that travel around the streets.

4 He looked really bored, with his e_ _ _ _s on the table and his head between his hands.

5 Wow! It's my first time on a plane! I've never f_ _ _ _ before today!

6 We were late, so we didn't c_ _ _ _ the train.

7 The dog was really hot – its t_ _ _ _ _ was hanging out of its mouth.

6 Circle the correct words.

Jake Hi, Mum. I've (been) / gone into town – and look! I've ¹buy / bought a new shirt.

Mum It's nice, Jake. But isn't it a bit small? You're tall and you've got big ²shoulders / ankles.

Jake No, Mum, it's fine. I think ³I wear / I'll wear it to Evie's party on Saturday.

Mum Oh, is she having a party?

Jake Yes, it's for her birthday. ⁴She's invited / She invites everyone from school.

Mum But her birthday ⁵was / has been last month!

Jake I know. But her mother was ill, so she couldn't have a party then.

Mum Oh, I'm sorry to ⁶know / hear that. Is her mother OK now?

Jake Oh, yes, she's ⁷being / doing OK. She had a problem with her ⁸stomach / knee – the doctors think she ⁹ate / has eaten something bad.

Mum Oh, ¹⁰sorry / poor Evie. Well, please tell her that I hope the party is great.

Jake Thanks, Mum. I'll tell her when I ¹¹see / will see her.

DIALOGUE

7 🔊 12.05 **Complete the conversation with words from the list. There are two that you don't need.**

> as soon as | been | doing | gone | hear | if
> knee | poor | shame | went | will | won't

Harvey Hi, Amber. Where have you ⁰ _been_ ?

Amber At the doctor's. I hurt my ¹_____ the other day.

Harvey Oh, I'm sorry to ²_____ that. Is everything OK now?

Amber Not really. I'll have to see him again ³_____ it doesn't get better.

Harvey ⁴_____ you.

Amber Oh, it's not so bad. It hurts a bit, but I'm ⁵_____ OK. Listen, I'm looking for Matt. Do you know where he is?

Harvey Oh, he isn't here. He's ⁶_____ to see his grandmother. She's ill. He ⁷_____ be back until about six o'clock.

Amber That's a ⁸_____ . I really want to talk to him. Can you ask him to call me, please?

Harvey Sure. I'll ask him ⁹_____ he gets back.

📖 READING

8 **Read the text about children and schools in Niger. Answer the questions.**

0 In Niger, what percentage of people have running water at home?

20% of people have running water at home.

1 Who often goes to get water for a family?

_____

2 Why is Sani often two hours late for school?

_____

3 Why does Badjeba sometimes fall asleep in lessons?

_____

4 Why do families send children to get water when it makes them late for school?

_____

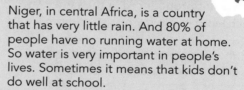

School or water?

Niger, in central Africa, is a country that has very little rain. And 80% of people have no running water at home. So water is very important in people's lives. Sometimes it means that kids don't do well at school.

Children are often the ones who have to find water for the family. They go out on donkeys and travel up to ten kilometres to get water. And then they are late for school, or they don't go at all. Sani, 11, gets water for his family in the morning and usually gets to school at 10 o'clock – two hours late. 'Some of the other children are lucky,' he says. 'They don't have to get water and so they learn more quickly than me.'

It's hard for the children to study. One girl, Badjeba, says, 'I get up at 4.30 to get water, five kilometres away. Then I take it home. Then I walk to school. I'm exhausted. I'm so tired that I fall asleep in the lessons. And after school, I have to go and find water again.'

In one classroom, the teacher asks: 'How many of you were late today because you had to get water?' And about 90% of the kids put their hand up. Their families send them to get water – school is important but water is life.

✏️ WRITING

9 **Imagine you are either Sani or Badjeba. Write a diary entry for a school day (about 100–120 words). Write about these things.**

- what you did before school
- what you did at school
- what you did after school

PRONUNCIATION

UNIT 7
Vowel sounds: /ʊ/ and /uː/

1 🔊 7.04 **What are you buying? Put your finger on
Start. Listen to the words. Go up if you hear the /ʊ/
sound and down if you hear the /uː/ sound. Say the
word at the end. You'll hear the words twice.**

   0   *Boots*
   1 _____
   2 _____
   3 _____
   4 _____
   5 _____

2 🔊 7.05 **Listen, check and repeat.**

3 **All of these words are written with the letters *oo*
but they are not pronounced in the same way.
Write each word in the /ʊ/ or /uː/ column.**

> choose | cook | cool | food
> good | l̶o̶o̶k̶ | school | stood

/ʊ/ – foot	/uː/ – room
look	

4 a **Which words rhyme with *should*?**

   _____ and _____ .

  b **Which word rhymes with *shoes*?** _____ .

5 🔊 7.06 **Listen, check and repeat.**

UNIT 8
Strong and weak forms of *was* and *were*

1 **Write *was*, *wasn't*, *were* or *weren't* to complete
the sentences.**

  1 A ____*Was*___ she happy to get her new bike?
    B Yes, she _____ . She loves it.
  2 A _____ they playing volleyball in the park?
    B No, they _____ . They _____ at
    the beach.
  3 A Look – that girl _____ at the pool yesterday.
    B No, she _____ !
    A Yes, she _____ ! She's a good swimmer.
    B She _____ . The girl we saw had long
    brown hair.

4 A They _____ very happy with the restaurant
   last night.
  B Really? Why not?
  A Because they _____ waiting for their food
   for a long time.

5 A _____ you at the football match last night?
  B No, I _____ . I _____ studying for an
   exam.
  A _____ you? So was I!

2 🔊 8.01 **Listen, check and repeat.**

3 **Circle the stressed forms of these verbs.**

4 🔊 8.01 **Listen again and check.**

UNIT 9
Vowel sounds: /ɪ/ and /aɪ/

1 **Write the words in the columns.**

> find | fine | g̶i̶v̶e̶ | gym | list | nice | night
> sing | smile | spring | style | thin | wild | wish

/ɪ/ – think	/aɪ/ – drive
give	

2 🔊 9.01 **Listen, check and repeat.**

3 **Match to make sentences.**

  0 (I'm) going to Keep Fit   a driving at night.
  1 Kim doesn't like   b has a healthy lifestyle.
  2 Lions and tigers   c ride our bikes.
  3 Mike exercises and   d classes at the gym.
  4 It's a nice day, so let's   e are happier in the wild.

4 🔊 9.02 **Listen and check.**

5 **Circle all of the words in the sentences with
the /aɪ/ sound.**

6 🔊 9.03 **Listen, check and repeat.**

UNIT 10
Voiced /ð/ and unvoiced /θ/ consonants

1 **Complete the sentences.**

> clothes | Earth | Maths | months | then
> ~~things~~ | think | third | Thursday | youth

0 There are so many _things_ to do in Sydney.

1 Let's go shopping. I want to buy some new _____ .

2 These three students came first, second and _____ in the race.

3 My father's birthday's on _____ .

4 We had dinner and _____ we went to the theatre.

5 I _____ we should go out to a restaurant tonight.

6 We must look after the _____ ; it's a beautiful planet.

7 There are twelve _____ in a year.

8 We've got a _____ class after the break.

9 A _____ is a young person.

2 🔊 **10.03** **Listen, check and repeat.**

3 Ⓒircle all the words in the sentences with a voiced *th* sound. <u>Underline</u> all the words with an unvoiced *th* sound.

UNIT 11
The /h/ consonant sound

1 **Complete the sentences with the words in the list.**

> hair | happy | healthy | hear | help
> here | ~~homework~~ | hospital | humans | hurt

0 I'll come to your house when I've finished my History _homework_ .

1 It's _____ to eat honey.

2 Harry had to go to the _____ in an ambulance.

3 That suitcase looks heavy. Can I _____ you carry it?

4 Helen's got beautiful long black _____ .

5 I couldn't _____ the music because the headphones weren't working.

6 I hope you'll be _____ in your new home.

7 In the future _____ won't have as much hair as they do now.

8 Hilary _____ her knee while she was running yesterday.

9 Can you come _____ and help me, please?

2 🔊 **11.01** **Listen, check and repeat.**

UNIT 12
Sentence stress

1 **Complete the sentences.**

> cooker | eggs | English | farmer
> island | laptop | ~~scarf~~ | taxi

0 I'm wearing a <u>shirt</u>, a <u>skirt</u>, a <u>hat</u> and a _scarf_ .

1 An artist, a doctor, a teacher and a _____ .

2 We've got Maths, then Art, then History and then _____ .

3 We need a desk, a lamp, a sofa and a _____ .

4 We caught a plane and then a train and then a bus and then a _____ .

5 We put in flour and sugar and then butter and _____ .

6 For sale: a digital camera, a pen drive, a microphone and a _____ .

7 We saw a lake, a river, a jungle and an _____ .

2 🔊 **12.01** **Listen, check and repeat.**

3 Underline the stressed words in the lists in Exercise 1.

4 🔊 **12.01** **Listen again, check and repeat.**

5 Look at the stressed words in the sentences 0–7. Then read and Ⓒircle the correct word to complete the rule.

> We generally stress words like [1]*nouns / articles* that give us information. We don't generally stress words like [2]*nouns / articles*.

GRAMMAR REFERENCE

UNIT 7
should / shouldn't

1 **When we want to say that something is a good idea (or is a bad idea), we can use *should* or *shouldn't*.**

   *I **should study** this weekend.* (I think it's a good idea.)
   *They **shouldn't buy** that car.* (I think it's a bad idea.)
   ***Should we go** out tonight?* (Do you think this is a good idea?)

2 ***Should* is a modal verb. We use *should* / *shouldn't* + base form of the verb, and the form is the same for all subjects. We don't use any form of *do* in the negative.**

   *I **should try** to study more.*
   *I **shouldn't watch** TV tonight.*

3 **Questions are formed with *should* + subject + base form of the verb. Again, we don't use any form of *do* in questions or short answers.**

   ***Should** I **ask** the teacher?*
   *Yes, you **should**. / No, you **shouldn't**.*

have to / don't have to

1 **We use *have to* to say that it is necessary or very important to do something.**

   *I'm late, I **have to go** now. We **have to be** at school at 8.30.*

   With a third person singular subject (*he, she, it*) we use *has to*.

   *Maggie is very ill – she **has to stay** in bed.*
   *My dad **has to go** to York tomorrow for a meeting.*

2 **We use the negative form *don't / doesn't have to* to say that it isn't necessary or important to do something.**

   *It's Sunday, so I **don't have to get up** early.*
   *She isn't late – she **doesn't have to hurry**.*

3 **We form questions with *do* or *does*.**

   ***Do** I **have to go** to the dentist?*
   ***Does** he **have to go** home now?*

4 **All forms of *have to* are followed by the base form of the verb.**

mustn't vs. don't have to

1 **We use *mustn't* to say that it is necessary or very important <u>not</u> to do something.**

   *You **mustn't be** late.   I **mustn't forget** to phone Jenny.*

2 ***Mustn't* has a different meaning from *don't / doesn't have to*.**

   *You **don't have to tell** your friends.* (It isn't necessary for you to tell them, but you can if you want to.)
   *You **mustn't tell** your friends.* (Don't tell your friends – it's a secret!)

UNIT 8
Past continuous

1 **We use the past continuous to talk about actions in progress at a certain time in the past.**

   *In 2012, we **were living** in the US.*
   *At 4 o'clock yesterday, I **was sitting** in a lesson.*
   *Last night, the TV was on, but I **wasn't watching** it.*

2 **The past continuous is formed with the past simple of *be* + verb + *-ing*.**

   *I **was reading** a book. I **wasn't enjoying** it.*
   *You **were running** very fast! But you **weren't winning**!*
   *Jo **was playing** computer games. She **wasn't studying**.*

3 **The question is formed with the past simple of *be* + subject + verb + *-ing*. Short answers are formed with *Yes / No* + pronoun + *was / were* or *wasn't / weren't*.**

   ***Was** James **running**? Yes, he **was**. / No, he **wasn't**.*
   *What **were** you **studying**?   Why **was** she **crying**?*

Past continuous vs. past simple

1 **When we talk about the past, we use the past simple for actions that happened at one particular time. We use the past continuous for background actions.**

   *When Alex **arrived**, I **was having** dinner.*
   *He **was running** very fast and he **didn't see** the tree.*

2 **We often use *when* with the past simple, and *while* with the past continuous.**

   *I was reading **when** the phone **rang**.*
   ***While** my father **was running**, he fell into a river.*

UNIT 9
Comparative adjectives

1 **When we want to compare two things, or two groups of things, we use a comparative form + *than*.**

   *I'm **older than** my brother.*
   *France is **bigger than** Britain.*

2 **With short adjectives, we normally add *-er*.**

   old ➜ *older*   *cheap* ➜ *cheaper*   *clever* ➜ *cleverer*

   If the adjective ends in *-e*, we only add *-r*.

   nice ➜ *nicer*   *safe* ➜ *safer*

If the adjective ends with consonant + -*y*, we change the -*y* to -*i* and add -*er*.

easy ➜ *easier*   *early* ➜ *earlier*   *happy* ➜ *happier*

If the adjective ends in a consonant + vowel + consonant, we double the final consonant and add -*er*.

big ➜ *bigger*   *sad* ➜ *sadder*   *thin* ➜ *thinner*

3   With longer adjectives (more than two syllables), we don't change the adjective – we put *more* in front of it.

expensive ➜ **more** *expensive*   *difficult* ➜ **more** *difficult*
interesting ➜ **more** *interesting*

4   Some adjectives are irregular – they have a different comparative form.

good ➜ **better**   *bad* ➜ **worse**   *far* ➜ **further**

Superlative adjectives

1   When we compare something with two or more other things, we use a superlative form with *the*.

*Steve is **the tallest** boy in our class.*
*Brazil is **the biggest** country in South America.*

2   With short adjectives, we normally add -*est*.

tall ➜ *the tallest*   *short* ➜ *the shortest*
old ➜ *the oldest*   *clean* ➜ *the cleanest*

Spelling rules for the -*est* ending are the same as for the -*er* ending in the comparative form.

nice ➜ *the nicest*   *happy* ➜ *the happiest*
safe ➜ *the safest*   *big* ➜ *the biggest*
easy ➜ *the easiest*   *thin* ➜ *the thinnest*

3   With longer adjectives (more than two syllables), we don't change the adjective – we put *the most* in front of it.

delicious ➜ **the most** *delicious*
important ➜ **the most** *important*
intelligent ➜ **the most** *intelligent*
*This is **the most important** day of my life.*

4   Some adjectives are irregular.

good ➜ **the best**   *bad* ➜ **the worst**   *far* ➜ **the furthest**
*Saturday is **the best** day of the week.*
*My team is **the worst** team in the world!*

can / can't (ability)

1   We use *can* / *can't* + the base form of the verb to talk about someone's ability to do something. The form of *can* / *can't* is the same for every person.

*My father **can lift** 100 kg.*   *I **can't lift** heavy things.*
*I **can swim** 5 kilometres.*   *My brother **can't swim**.*

2   To make questions, we use *Can* + subject + base form of the verb. Short answers are formed with *Yes / No* + pronoun + *can* or *can't*.

*Can your sister **swim**?   **Yes**, she **can**.*
*Can you **lift** 50 kilos?   **No**, I **can't**.*

UNIT 10
be going to for plans and intentions

1   We use *be going to* to talk about things we intend to do in the future.

*I'm **going to visit** my grandfather tomorrow.*
*My sister's **going to study** German at university.*

2   The form is the present simple of *be* + *going to* + base form of the verb.

*I'm **going to stay** at home on Sunday. I'm **not going to go** out.*
*She's **going to look** around the shops. She **isn't going to buy** anything.*
*Are you **going to watch** the film?*
*Is he **going to give** us homework tonight?*

3   Short answers are formed using *Yes / No* + pronoun + the correct form of *be* (positive or negative).

Present continuous for future arrangements

We can use the present continuous to talk about arrangements for the future.

*We're **having** a party next weekend. (It's organised.)*
*I'm **meeting** my friends in the park tomorrow. (I talked to my friends and we agreed to meet.)*
*Our parents **are going** on holiday to Spain next month. (They have their airline tickets and hotel reservation.)*

Adverbs

1   Adverbs usually go with verbs – they describe an action.

*We **walked** home **slowly**.   The train **arrived late**.*
***Drive carefully**!*

2   A lot of adverbs are formed by adjective + -*ly*.

quiet ➜ *quietly*   *bad* ➜ *badly*   *polite* ➜ *politely*

If the adjective ends in -*le*, we drop the -*e* and add -*y*.

terrible ➜ *terribly*   *comfortable* ➜ *comfortably*

If the adjective ends in consonant + -*y*, we change the -*y* to -*i* and add -*ly*.

easy ➜ *easily*   *happy* ➜ *happily*   *lucky* ➜ *luckily*

3   Some adverbs are irregular – they don't have an -*ly* ending.

good ➜ **well**   *fast* ➜ **fast**   *hard* ➜ **hard**
early ➜ **early**   *late* ➜ **late**
*I played **well** last week.   He worked **hard** all day.*
*She ran very **fast**.*

4   Adverbs usually come immediately after the verb, or, if the verb has an object, after the object.

*She **sings well**.   She **plays the piano well**.*

UNIT 11
will / won't for future predictions

1 We use *will* (*'ll*) and *won't* to make predictions about the future.

When I'm older, I'll travel round the world.
I won't stay here!
I'm sure you'll pass the test tomorrow. The questions won't be very difficult.
In the future, people will take holidays on Mars. But people won't live there.

2 We use *will* / *won't* + base form of the verb, and the form is the same for all subjects. We don't use any form of *do* in the negative.

You'll pass the test.   You won't pass the test.
He'll pass the test.   He won't pass the test.

3 Questions are formed with *will* + subject + base form of the verb. Again, we don't use any form of *do* in questions or short answers.

Will Andrea go to university?
Yes, she will. / No, she won't.
Will your friends come to the party?
Yes, they will. / No, they won't.

First conditional

1 In conditional sentences there are two clauses, an *if* clause and a result clause. We use the first conditional when it is possible or likely that the situation in the *if* clause will happen in the future.

If I pass the test, my parents will be happy.
(It's possible that I will pass, but I'm not sure.)
If it doesn't rain, we'll go for a walk. (Perhaps it will rain, but I'm not sure.)

2 The *if* clause is formed with *if* + subject + present simple. The result clause is formed with subject + *will* + base form of the verb. There is a comma after the *if* clause.

If we have time, we'll do some shopping.
If you don't start your homework soon, you won't finish it tonight.

3 We can change the order of the two clauses. In this case, there is no comma between the clauses.

We'll do some shopping if we have time.
You won't finish your homework tonight if you don't start it soon.

Time clauses with when / as soon as

In sentences about the future, we use the present tense after *when* or *as soon as*, and the *will* future in the main clause.

When I'm 18, I'll go to university.
I'll call you as soon as I get there.

UNIT 12
Present perfect simple with ever / never

1 We often use the present perfect to talk about things from the beginning of our life until now.

Sandro has travelled to a lot of different countries.
(from when he was born until now)
I haven't met your parents. (at any time in my life, from when I was born until now)

2 When we use the present perfect with this meaning, we often use *ever* (*at any time in someone's life*) in questions, and *never* (*not ever*) in sentences. *Ever* comes between the noun or pronoun and the past participle. *Never* comes immediately after *have* / *has*.

Have you ever eaten Thai food?
I've never been interested in cooking.

3 The present perfect is formed with the present tense of *have* + past participle of the main verb.
For regular verbs, the past participle has the same *-ed* ending as the past simple. Irregular verbs have different past participles.

Regular verbs
We've stayed in Athens three times.
Have they ever climbed a mountain?

Irregular verbs
We've been there three times.
Have they ever flown in a plane?

See page 128 for the past participles of irregular verbs.

4 There is a difference between *been* and *gone*.

I've been to the supermarket. (I went to the supermarket and now I am back again.)
They've gone to the supermarket. (They went to the supermarket and they are still there.)

Present perfect vs. past simple

Both the present perfect and the past simple refer to the past. But we use the past simple to talk about situations or actions at a particular time in the past. We use the present perfect to talk about situations or actions in the past that took place at an unspecified time between the past and now.

Past simple
I ate sushi two weeks ago.
I read a Shakespeare play last month.
He was late for school yesterday.

Present perfect
I've eaten sushi a lot of times.
I've read six Shakespeare plays.
He's been late to school four times.

IRREGULAR VERBS

Base form	Past simple	Past participle
be	was / were	been
become	became	become
begin	began	begun
break	broke	broken
bring	brought	brought
build	built	built
buy	bought	bought
can	could	–
catch	caught	caught
choose	chose	chosen
come	came	come
cost	cost	cost
cut	cut	cut
do	did	done
draw	drew	drawn
drink	drank	drunk
drive	drove	driven
eat	ate	eaten
fall	fell	fallen
feel	felt	felt
find	found	found
fly	flew	flown
forget	forgot	forgotten
get	got	got
give	gave	given
go	went	gone
grow	grew	grown
have	had	had
hear	heard	heard
hit	hit	hit
keep	kept	kept
know	knew	known
leave	left	left

Base form	Past simple	Past participle
lend	lent	lent
lie	lay	lain
lose	lost	lost
make	made	made
mean	meant	meant
meet	met	met
pay	paid	paid
put	put	put
read /riːd/	read /red/	read /red/
ride	rode	ridden
run	ran	run
say	said	said
see	saw	seen
sell	sold	sold
send	sent	sent
show	showed	shown
sing	sang	sung
sit	sat	sat
sleep	slept	slept
speak	spoke	spoken
spend	spent	spent
stand	stood	stood
swim	swam	swum
take	took	taken
teach	taught	taught
tell	told	told
think	thought	thought
throw	threw	thrown
understand	understood	understood
wake	woke	woken
wear	wore	worn
win	won	won
write	wrote	written

ACKNOWLEDGEMENTS

Acknowledgements

The authors and publishers acknowledge the following sources of copyright material and are grateful for the permissions granted. While every effort has been made, it has not always been possible to identify the sources of all the material used, or to trace all copyright holders. If any omissions are brought to our notice, we will be happy to include the appropriate acknowledgements on reprinting and in the next update to the digital edition, as applicable.

Key: U = Unit.

Text

U7: Joshua Silver for the text about him. Reproduced with kind permission; Kenneth Shinozuka for the text about him. Reproduced with kind permission.

Photographs

All the photographs are sourced from Getty Images.

U7: artisteer/iStock/Getty Images Plus; by_nicholas/E+; deepblue4you/E+; macbrianmun/iStock/Getty Images Plus; dashadima/iStock/Getty Images Plus; koya79/iStock/Getty Images Plus; The Washington Post; India Herlem/EyeEm; Roman_Gorielov/iStock/Getty Images Plus; Sheryl Saniel/EyeEm; Nnehring; Tetra Images; fullvalue/E+; **U8:** PieroAnnoni/iStock/Getty Images Plus; Laurence Mouton/PhotoAlto Agency RF Collections; Henry Georgi/Corbis; Astrakan Images/Cultura; Mike Powell/The Image Bank/Getty Images Plus; Hirun Laowisit/EyeEm; SchulteProductions/iStock/Getty Images Plus; skodonnell/E+; Trio Images/Photodisc; Michael Blann/Photodisc; BraunS/iStock/Getty Images Plus; Luc Beziat/Photographer's Choice/Getty Images Plus; LightFieldStudios/iStock/Getty Images Plus; bjeayes/iStock/Getty Images Plus; Petershort/iStock/Getty Images Plus; Givaga/iStock/Getty Images Plus; sarah5/iStock/Getty Images Plus; ddukang/iStock/Getty Images Plus; Floortje/iStock/Getty Images Plus; technotr/E+; Keystone/Stringer/Hulton Archive; Central Press/Stringer/Hulton Archive; Tony Duffy/Staff/Getty Images Sport; Michael DeYoung; Matthias Tunger/The Image Bank/Getty Images Plus; FatCamera/E+; Adie Bush/Cultura; LuckyBusiness/iStock/Getty Images Plus; Stuart Gregory/Photodisc; Buena Vista Images/DigitalVision; svarshik/iStock Editorial/Getty Images Plus; travenian/iStock/Getty Images Plus; Jupiterimages/Stockbyte; Carol Yepes/Moment; SteveAllenPhoto/iStock Editorial/Getty Images Plus; Jung Yeon-JE/Staff/AFP; **U9:** mammuth/E+; Amaia Arozena & Gotzon Iraola/Moment; matthewleesdixon/iStock/Getty Images Plus; Knaupe/E+; spooh/E+; Serg_Velusceac/iStock/Getty Images Plus; Ralph Adolphs/500px; PhotoStock-Israel/Cultura; VargaJones/iStock/Getty Images Plus; Anna Henly/Oxford Scientific/Getty Images Plus; John W Banagan/Lonely Planet Images/Getty Images Plus; **U10:** Barcin/iStock/Getty Images Plus; Caiaimage/Sam Edwards; BrianAJackson/iStock/Getty Images Plus; Daria Botieva/Eyeem; Richard Newstead/Moment; Aleksandrs Goldobenkovs/iStock/Getty Images Plus; Laurence Dutton/Stone/Getty Images Plus; Phil Friar/iStock/Getty Images Plus; Claver Carroll/Photolibrary/Getty Images Plus; Gideon Mendel/Contributor/Corbis Historical; Rich Jones Photography/Moment; Philipp Walter/EyeEm; **U11:** XiXinXing; yacobchuk/iStock/Getty Images Plus; Eric Audras/Onoky; Damir Khabirov/iStock/Getty Images Plus; Lammeyer/iStock/Getty Images Plus; RunPhoto/DigitalVision; energyy/iStock/Getty Images Plus; m-imagephotography/Stock/Getty Images Plus; velvelvel/iStock/Getty Images Plus; PeopleImages/E+; Guido Mieth/DigitalVision; Donald Iain Smith/Photodisc; Saturated/iStock/Getty Images Plus; The Asahi Shimbun; Janine Lamontagne/E+; gbh007/iStock/Getty Images Plus; **U12:** william87/iStock/Getty Images Plus; m-imagephotography/iStock/Getty Images Plus; kruwt/iStock/Getty Images Plus; Image Source; MarioGuti/iStock/Getty Images Plus; Paul Biris/Moment; Solidago/E+; gbh007/iStock/Getty Images Plus; sharply_done/iStock/Getty Images Plus; deimagine/E+; MStudioImages/E+.

The following image is sourced from other source/library:

U7: Copyright © 2019 SafeWander.

Illustrations

Dusan Lakicevic (Beehive Illustration) p. 70; Emma Nyari (Beehive Illustration) pp. 66, 91, 112; Lisa Reed (The Bright Agency) pp. 73, 108; Tom Heard (The Bright Agency) pp. 82, 101, 111; Michael McCabe (Beehive Illustration) p. 88; Adam Linley (Beehive Illustration) pp. 64, 92; Martin Sanders (Beehive Illustration) pp. 93, 114.

Grammar Rap video stills: Silversun Media Group.